Government

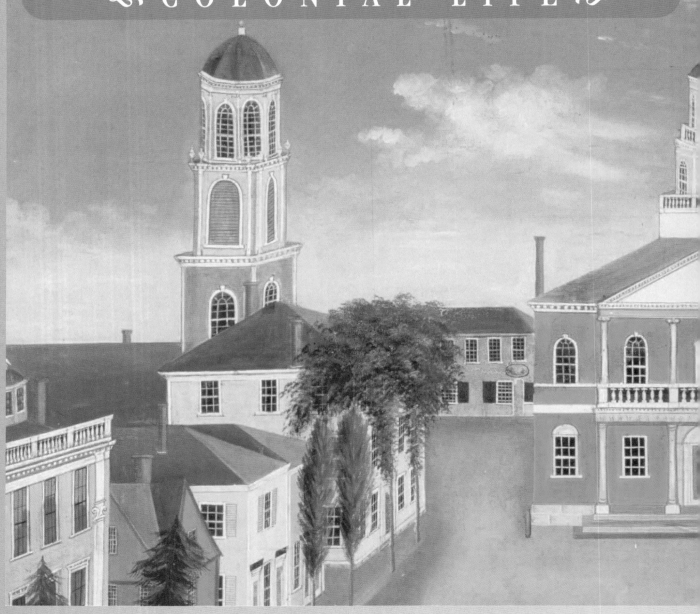

❧ COLONIAL LIFE ❧

Government

Martin Kelly and Melissa Kelly

Sharpe Focus
an imprint of M.E. Sharpe, Inc.

Sharpe Focus
An imprint of M.E. Sharpe, Inc.
80 Business Park Drive
Armonk, NY 10504
www.mesharpe.com

ISBN: 978-0-7656-8112-6

Library of Congress Cataloging-in-Publication Data

Library of Congress Cataloging-in-Publication Data

Kelly, Martin, 1971-
  Government / Martin and Melissa Kelly.
      p. cm. — (Colonial life)
  Includes bibliographical references and index.
  ISBN 978-0-7656-8112-6 (hardcover : alk. paper)
  1. United States—Politics and government—To 1775—Juvenile literature.
  2. Europe—Colonies—America—Administration—Juvenile literature.
  I. Kelly, Melissa. II. Title.

E188.K275 2008
973.2—dc22

2007007845

Editor: Peter Mavrikis
Program Coordinator: Cathleen Prisco
Production Manager: Laura Brengelman
Editorial Assistant: Alison Morretta
Design: Charles Davey LLC, Book Productions

Printed in Malaysia

9 8 7 6 5 4 3 2 1

Photo and Map Credits: Cover: page 85: Atwater Kent Museum of Philadelphia / Bridgeman Art Library; title page: © Peabody Essex Museum, Salem, Massachusetts / Bridgeman Art Library; half title: ©Pennsylvania Academy of the Fine Arts, Philadelphia, USA / The Bridgeman Art Library; page 15: Bildarchiv Preussischer Kulturbesitz / Art Resource, NY; page 25: HIP / Art Resource, NY; pages 6–7: Réunion des Musées Nationaux / Art Resource, NY; page 32: Smithsonian American Art Museum, Washington, DC / Art Resource, NY; pages 45, 48, 76: © Collection of the New-York Historical Society, USA / The Bridgeman Art Library; page 21: © Peabody Essex Museum, Salem, Massachusetts / Bridgeman Art Library; pages 62–63: ©Courtesy of the Council, National Army Museum, London, UK / The Bridgeman Art Library; page 9: ©Library of Congress, Washington D.C., USA / The Bridgeman Art Library; pages 38–39: ©Museum of Fine Arts, Houston, Texas, USA / Hogg Brothers Collection, Gift of Miss Ima Hogg / The Bridgeman Art Library; page 36: ©Pennsylvania Academy of the Fine Arts, Philadelphia, USA / The Bridgeman Art Library; page 88: ©Pennsylvania State Capitol, PA, USA / The Bridgeman Art Library; page 46: ©Service Historique de la Marine, Vincennes, France / Lauros / Giraudon / The Bridgeman Art Library; pages 72, 85: Atwater Kent Museum of Philadelphia / Bridgeman Art Library; page 41: Chichén Itzá, Yucatán State, Mexico / Bridgeman Art Library; page 57: Florence Griswold Museum, Old Lyme, Connecticut / Gift of the Hartford Steam Boiler Inspection & Inusrance Company / Bridgeman Art Library; page 17: Giraudon / Bridgeman Art Library; page 23: Guildhall Library, Corporation of London, United Kingdom / Bridgeman Art Library; page 35: Museum of Fine Arts, Boston / Bridgeman Art Library; page 11: Private Collection / Bridgeman Art Library; page 65: Private Collection / Philip Mould, Historical Portraits Ltd., London, United Kingdom / Bridgeman Art Library; page 61: The Stapleton Colletion / Bridgeman Art Library; pages 54, 87: Brown Brothers; pages 12, 19, 29, 42, 47, 69, 77, 83: Cartographics; page 30: Courtesy of Enoch Pratt Free Library, Central Library / State Library Resource Center, Baltimore, Maryland; page 73: Fort Necessity National Park; pages 50–51: Hulton Archive / Getty Images; pages 27, 70: MPI / Stringer / Hulton Archive / Getty Images; pages 18, 40, 48, 66, 82, 89, back cover: Stock Montage / Hulton Archive / Getty Images; page 53: Time & Life Pictures / Stringer / Getty Images; pages 68, 74: Library of Congress; page 33: New York Public Library.

Contents ❧

The French navigator and explorer Jacques Cartier was the first European to explore and map the St. Lawrence River. This knowledge of the river helped the French establish a colonial presence in Canada.

CHAPTER ONE ❧
Colonial Rule

THE FIRST EUROPEAN KNOWN TO HAVE landed in North America was the Norseman Leif Eiriksson. He lived between 980 and 1020 C.E. and founded settlements in present-day Newfoundland. He named the land Vinland after the wild grapes found there. However, he and his men were not the first inhabitants of the New World. North and South America were peopled by numerous tribes and, in some cases, established civilizations of Native Americans. The arrival of Europeans would alter the land and the life that the Native Americans had established. Eiriksson's expedition was the first of many by Europeans.

The Push to Colonize

The real push to explore lands to the west of Europe was motivated by the desire to find a quick route to the Far East. In 1271, Marco Polo arrived in China with his father on a diplomatic mission. They had traveled by land across Asia. He lived at the court of the Mongol conqueror Kublai Khan for over twenty years. Upon his return to Italy, he wrote a famous book, *The Travels of Marco Polo*. This book and its description of China's riches captured the imagination of many future explorers including Christopher Columbus.

Land routes between Europe and China provided merchants with a way to trade for exotic items like spices and silk. However, the trip was difficult and took a long time. Traders who lived in western Europe and wished to trade with China had to travel through neighboring countries

Early Explorers

Date	Explorer	Nationality	Most Known For
Around 1000 C.E.	Leif Eiriksson	Norse	First European to reach North America.
1492–1504	Christopher Columbus	Italian	Four voyages to the Caribbean and West Indies.
1497–1498	Vasco da Gama	Portuguese	First to travel to North America by going around Africa.
1513	Vasco Nuñez de Balboa	Spanish	First European to sight the Pacific Ocean.
1519–1521	Hernán Cortés	Spanish	Conquered the Aztec.
1520–1521	Ferdinand Magellan	Portuguese	First European to circumnavigate the globe.
1532	Francisco Pizarro	Spanish	Conquered the Inca.
1534–1542	Jacques Cartier	French	Traveled the St. Lawrence River.
1539–1541	Hernando de Soto	Spanish	Discovered the Mississippi River.
1577–1580	Sir Francis Drake	English	First Englishman to sail around the world. He also led the English in the defeat of the Spanish Armada (1588).
1608	Samuel de Champlain	French	Founded Quebec.
1673	Jacques Marquette and Louis Joliet	French	Explored the Mississippi River.
1682	René-Robert Cavelier	French	Explored the Mississippi to its mouth at New Orleans and claimed it for France.

that were often hostile. Their only hope of successfully trading with the Far East was by sea. In an attempt to find a sea route to China, the Portuguese first tried to go east. They headed down around the continent of Africa and sailed around the Cape of Good Hope, at Africa's most southern point. This allowed them to arrive in India and continue their travels. However, this too was a difficult and dangerous trip. The Spanish saw the Portuguese efforts and successes and decided to sponsor their own explorations. They hoped to find an even quicker and easier route to the Far East.

An Italian named Christopher Columbus decided to try to find a route to China by sailing west. He tried to get the Portuguese to pay for his trip first. When this failed, he turned to King Ferdinand and Queen Isabella of Spain. In 1492, they agreed to fund his voyage.

Columbus left with his crew and three ships, the *Niña*, *Pinta*, and *Santa Maria*, to find the route to the Far East. However, he had miscalculated the earth's circumference. When he did find land, he thought that he had found the Indies. Instead, he had reached North America. His error led to his calling the natives he found there Indians.

From these beginnings, four major European nations began to explore and colonize the New World they had found: Spain, France, the Netherlands, and England. Each was motivated first and foremost by economic reasons. At the same time, each nation had their own methods for settling in the new lands.

Queen Isabella and King Ferdinand of Spain bid Christopher Columbus farewell as he departs on his first voyage. A priest blesses the men who are preparing to leave on the ships that wait in the background.

Spanish Colonization

The Spanish were the first to set up major settlements in North and South America. The conquistadors (con-KEE-stah-dors), or Spanish soldiers, had three main objectives: gold, glory, and God. They came to the New World to plunder it for its riches. As they began to interact with the native population, many saw evidence of gold or other forms of wealth. In fact, the easy manner with which these items were treated by the natives made the Spanish believe that they were readily available.

The conquests of the Aztec people, by Hernán Cortés, and the Peruvian Inca, by Francisco Pizarro, fed the belief that the New

World was rife with riches. The conquistadors desperately desired conquest to gain glory for the Spanish court. This combination of conquest and the gold that was sent back to Spain led to further missions. It also spurred the desire of other European nations to send their own explorers and colonizers to America.

Without realizing it, the Spanish spread death with their arrival because of the diseases they carried. The native people had little or no immunity to common European illnesses. While many of the Spanish had become immune to smallpox, they could still carry the disease and pass it on to the native people. The death toll from this and other diseases was so great that some historians estimate that more than 90 percent of the native population was killed in some areas.

The Spanish treated the native peoples with disdain. They sent missionaries to the Americas, along with the conquistadors, with the goal of converting the natives to Catholicism. In many instances if the natives did not convert, they were treated as heathens, or uncivilized nonbelievers, and some conquistadors believed that this meant they were permitted to hurt or kill the natives. The Catholic Church at that time considered the conversion of the native populations not only a Christian duty but also as the only way to save the souls of the newly discovered peoples. Despite the typical treatment by the conquistadors, many Catholic missionaries became staunch defenders of the native peoples when they saw the way they were being treated.

A Flat Earth? &

Despite the popular myth, Christopher Columbus was not the first person to believe or prove that the earth was round. The belief that the earth was round was known even in ancient times. Aristotle argued that it was round because of the shadow cast by it on the moon. It was this belief that the earth was spherical that caused Columbus to believe that if he sailed west he could reach the Far East by sea. His mistake was that he thought the earth was much smaller than it is, which led him to believe that he had reached the Indies when he had in fact landed in the Caribbean.

Spanish colonies were set up around a colonial governor with large landholders who had much power. The conquistadors would be given lands and also *encomiendas*. The encomienda system gave them the ability to tax native people and villages within a particular territory in exchange for protection. The individual workers, in this case the Indians, technically owned their land but also owed the *encomendero* money or goods in exchange for military protection. By the early 1500s in many areas of the West Indies, almost all of the native people were dead through conquest or more often by disease. To replace those workers the Spanish began to import slaves from Africa.

In the southwestern United States, the Spanish settlements were generally focused around Franciscan or Jesuit missions. Missionaries would come into an area and begin converting Indians to Christianity. Towns would spring up around the missions, and inhabitants actually gained Spanish citizenship. Soldiers were sent to protect the towns.

At the time England was just building up its colonies, Spain already owned most of southern and central North America. They also controlled much of the territory in the present-day United States. The

The Spanish explorer Hernando de Soto is credited with being the first European to "discover" the Mississippi River. During his exploration of North America, De Soto's treatment of the native people was extremely cruel.

viceroyalty of Spain was centered in Mexico. Unlike England and France, the focus of Spanish colonization was mostly on the southern part of North America and much of Central and South America. The lands that the Spanish held in North America served a defensive purpose. They protected the trading empire that was booming to the south.

The reason for Spanish colonization was mostly to send money back home. The Spanish generally did not create self-sustaining economies that traded with the Native Americans for essentials. Their goals were different from those of the French and especially the English. This can be seen in the failure of the Spanish North American colonies to survive.

Introduction of African Slavery ✍

In 1501, the Spanish imported the first African slaves to the Americas. They were sent to Santo Domingo to replace the workforce of native people who had died from violence or disease. In the English colonies, the first Africans were listed in the service of planters in Jamestown in the year 1619, although at first most Africans who were brought to the English colonies worked as indentured servants, not slaves. By 1641, Massachusetts became the first British colony to legally recognize slavery. The slave trade continued to grow in the Americas throughout the seventeenth and eighteenth centuries.

French Colonization

Just like the Spanish, the French were also hoping to increase their wealth. Not only did they wish to gain from riches found within the New World but they also wanted to find a Northwest Passage that would lead to the Far East. This would allow a more direct, and thus quicker, trade route. In 1524, Giovanni da Verrazano, an Italian, was sent by the French to search for a passage to Asia, but he only found the coast of present-day Maine before turning back.

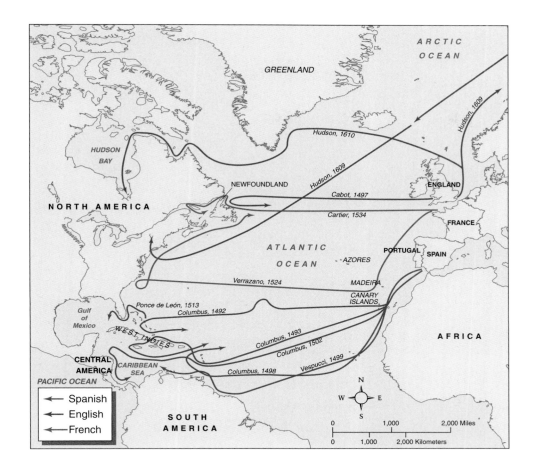

This map shows the routes that explorers charted across the Atlantic Ocean between 1492 and 1610. The Spanish mainly traveled to the south, while the English and the French spent time mainly in the north.

Ten years later, the French began to send groups to colonize the land they had found. Jacques Cartier was a French explorer who made three journeys to North America. He explored down the St. Lawrence River as far as present-day Montreal where he discovered that he could travel no further. Even though the French never found the Northwest Passage, they did lay claim to many parts of present-day Canada. However, they did not truly form permanent colonies until the early 1600s with the travels of Samuel de Champlain.

Samuel de Champlain explored farther into Canada and founded the city of Quebec. He had seen the importance of setting up a trading post with the Indians on the St. Lawrence River. French missionaries had accompanied him on his travels. They and the French

This image is of the Market Square in Veracruz, Mexico. The governor had a great deal of wealth and power, as evidenced by the huge Governor's Palace seen on the left. It was built in 1780.

settlers took a different approach toward the native population than did the Spanish. They were more likely to live among the native peoples as opposed to subjugating them. The missionaries, while wishing to convert the Indians, also allowed them to keep their own culture intact—unlike the Spanish.

Champlain became friends with the Montagnais (mon-tun-YA) Indians on the St. Lawrence River. He joined with them, the Algonquin (al-GON-kwin), and the Huron to fight against the Iroquois Confederacy. During one battle against the Iroquois he was severely wounded. Because of his relations with the Native Americans, he was able to make favorable trade agreements with them and formed his own trading company in 1615. Yet despite Champlain's best efforts, the French back home did not spend the time needed to make sure that Quebec did well, and the settlement was in danger of failing.

Typically, the French home authorities did not get deeply involved in the administration of the colonies, leaving this to those settling the area. However, the goal of this exploration and of French settlements in general was to create trading posts rather than permanent colonies. The French crown viewed ventures in North America as a way to increase France's wealth, following the theory of mercantilism, which stated that the only way to gain wealth was to explore and expand one's own money-making efforts. These trading posts traded for fur, which the traders sent back to France. French trading posts and settlements were ruled by a royally appointed governor called a viceroy. The success or failure of the colonies depended on the skill of the viceroy in governing the territory. It took the concentrated efforts of Champlain and Henri II, the Duke of Montmorency, who was the viceroy of New France from 1620 to 1625, to help Quebec eventually thrive.

In 1682, King Louis XIV sent René-Robert Cavelier de La Salle to explore from Canada down the Mississippi River as far as it would go. When La Salle got to the end of the river, where present-day New Orleans is, he claimed all of the Mississippi River basin for France and called it Louisiana. This area would remain in French hands until the Louisiana Purchase, in 1803, when President Thomas Jefferson bought the land for the United States.

Dutch Colonization

As with the other countries, the Dutch were interested in finding a Northwest Passage to the Indies to speed up their trade routes. In fact, the Dutch East India Company had a monopoly on trade with India and China in the early 1600s. The company hired Henry Hudson to find a Northwest Passage. He did not succeed in finding such a passage, but he did find Delaware Bay. He traveled up the Hudson River where he met some Iroquois Indians. This initial meeting allowed the Dutch to set up a positive trading partnership with the Iroquois. The Dutch built trading posts in the New World to trade with the native population for fur. Like the French, the Dutch traders' goal was to send furs and wealth back to the mother country. By 1621, the Dutch West India Company had a monopoly to trade with the New World. The company wished to create permanent settlements. Its goal was to create a colony called New Netherland that would be a province of the Netherlands. In 1626, Peter Minuit purchased the island of Manhattan, including the area where there was already a settlement referred to as New Amsterdam, from the Native Americans for what in today's terms would be $24.

In 1629, the Dutch West India Company created a system for settlement. It provided land called a patroonship to those who had fifty people to settle it within four years. The patroon (pat-ROON) was responsible for providing buildings and tools. The tenants paid rent to the patroon and lived by his laws. This system was very similar to that of feudalism where serfs paid for the right to have the lord's protection and land to work. Finding individuals who wanted to be tied to a lord in the New World was hard. Permanent colonization attempts were not widespread.

For the territory that the Dutch controlled, the company installed a governor who had almost complete control. Peter Stuyvesant became the governor of New Amsterdam in 1645. His rule was resented by the colonists. They forced him to create an advisory board similar to what the Dutch used in the Netherlands, but Stuyvesant remained in charge. Among his accomplishments, he added New Sweden to the realm of New Netherland. New Sweden had been settled in 1637 by the New Sweden Company with Germans, Swedes, and Dutch as stockholders. Peter Minuit was responsible for settling the New Sweden Company's first colony in the New World. The company's foothold in North America ended with this conquest by Stuyvesant.

Peter Stuyvesant was the last and most colorful governor of New Netherland. He established strong regulations for economic and social activities, created a small, primitive police force, and developed a basic educational system in several communities within the Dutch colony.

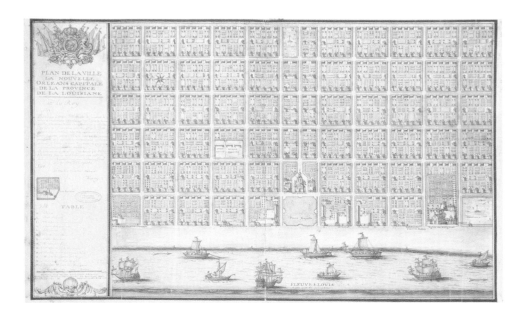

This map of the French city of New Orleans shows how well planned it was. Military engineers laid out the city in 1718, creating a clear plan for development. Louisiana remained in the hands of the French until 1803.

In 1664 English troops threatened to attack New Netherland. King Charles II had promised the lands to his brother James, Duke of York, if he could conquer them. When the English arrived, Stuyvesant asked the colonists to help defend the colony. Instead, the colonists pressured Stuyvesant to surrender, and he gave up New Amsterdam to the English without a fight. New Amsterdam then became known as New York. This event led to outright war between the Dutch and the English. In the treaty that ended the war, the Dutch gave up all claims to New Netherland in the New World.

English Colonization

The English were spurred on to explore and colonize the New World for two main reasons. First, they were interested in gaining some of the wealth that other Europeans had found in the Americas. Joint-stock companies, similar to modern corporations, were created to fund colonization. Investors pooled their money to send groups to the New World in the hopes of getting huge returns.

Second, people left England to colonize because they wanted more than they could get at home. They desired available land or, in many cases, religious freedom. England was overpopulated and experiencing the Protestant Reformation. Many individuals were willing to move to the New World to find land and build their own fortunes. Further, individuals emigrated to find religious freedoms they were denied at home. Due to these factors, the English more than any other national group were interested in creating permanent settlements in North America.

Normally, the English tolerated the native people as long as they did not act aggressively or interfere with their colonization attempts. However, many clashes occurred over the years between the English and the Native Americans as the colonists expanded along the eastern coastline.

Motivation

The main goal of all nations who explored in and colonized North, Central, and South America was wealth. Secondarily, the Spanish and French were also interested in converting the native population to Roman Catholicism. Individuals who colonized North America for England were also motivated by the desire to find land and freedom.

Each group had a different method for setting up colonies. The Spanish spread quickly and set up smaller settlements throughout the central and southern part of North America. At the same time they subjugated native populations along the way. The French created smaller trading posts where they could work with the native populations to trade for fur, which they sent back home. Their lands were

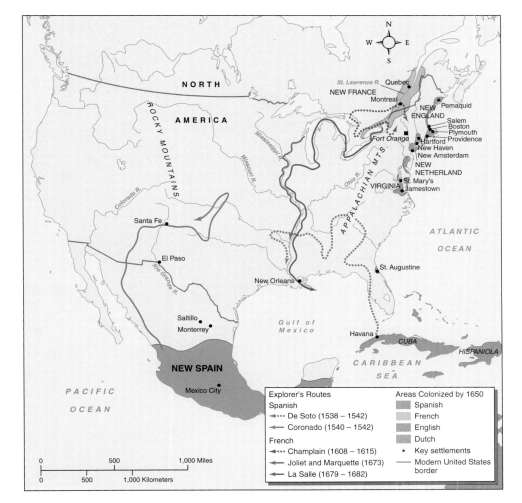

This map shows the North American routes of French and Spanish explorers between 1500 and 1700. It also provides an overview of the areas colonized by the four key powers (France, England, the Netherlands, and Spain) by 1650. Notice how the British and the Dutch focused on the Atlantic seaboard, while the French spent their time in the interior of North America, and the Spanish focused on the south.

mainly in present-day Canada and along the Mississippi River. The Dutch were interested at first in finding a way to the Indies but once this did not happen, they wanted to create a province in North America. Finally, the English were motivated to create permanent colonies in America due to the desire for greater riches, the pressure of increasing population, and the need of many to find freedom to practice their own religious beliefs. Because their focus was, in the end, permanent colonization, the English made the greatest inroads in settling the New World. Their governmental systems are the focus of much of the rest of this book.

Salem, Massachusetts, was settled in 1626, and its name was taken from the Hebrew word shalom, meaning peace. The town was founded by Puritans who were nonseparatists, which means that they never truly separated from the Church of England. In the early 1690s, Salem became the site of the largest witch hunt and trials in American history.

CHAPTER TWO

English Colonial Government

ENGLAND, LIKE ALL THE OTHER MAJOR

European powers in the sixteenth century, primarily started exploring and colonizing the New World to gain wealth. Once it became less likely that sea passage to the Far East was a possibility, these European countries turned their attention toward the lands they had found. Spain's successes with finding riches in its conquest of the Aztec and the Inca became well known. The English crown not only funded its own voyages across the Atlantic but also secretly supported pirates who preyed on Spanish galleons. However, the Spanish still held preeminence over the seas. Before the English could become a naval powerhouse, they had to deal with the Spanish.

By 1588, the Spanish had the strongest navy of all European nations. When Queen Elizabeth I of England had her cousin, the Catholic Mary, Queen of Scots, put to death, King Philip II of Spain was deeply offended. He was a staunch Catholic and decided to send his large fleet of ships, called the Armada, to attack Protestant England. Surprisingly, the Armada was defeated by the English navy. One of the main reasons for the Armada's defeat was that the Spanish ships were not as easy to maneuver as the smaller English ships. To add insult to injury, many of the surviving Spanish ships were destroyed by a large storm as they sailed home. Upon its victory, the English navy became known as the "Mistress of the Seas." It controlled the Atlantic Ocean without fearing the Spanish.

Two Main Motivations for Colonization

The English were motivated to colonize North America for two main reasons. Most important to the crown and the joint-stock companies was gaining wealth. They wanted to increase their riches and find new outlets for trade. Second, many who came to colonize North America desired freedom. Some, because of the increase in population and overcrowding back home, came to the New World so they could own their own land. Others wanted religious freedom in order to worship as they pleased.

Monetary Motivation

The main royal motivation for colonizing the New World was monetary. The English crown sought riches, so it funded expeditions to the New World. Similarly, Englishmen who wanted to have a part of the wealth they thought would be found funded personal colonization efforts through endeavors like the joint-stock companies. Both the crown and the companies expected colonies, once they were estab-

State-Sponsored Pirate 🙠

Sir Francis Drake was a privateer who preyed on Spanish ships as they crossed the Atlantic Ocean. While the Spanish considered him a pirate, the English supported his efforts and saw him as a privateer. He was a favorite of Queen Elizabeth I, in fact. In one of his most famous escapades, he raided Spanish ships near present-day Panama and captured a fortune in gold, which he took back to England. Drake was knighted by Elizabeth I aboard his ship the *Golden Hind* in 1581.

lished, to send back raw materials and items (including fur, wood, tar, foodstuffs, and wine) that would bring them profits and wealth. Later, they found that one of their largest money-making crops was tobacco.

The first major example of a company sending a group of colonists to the New World was the Virginia Company's Jamestown experiment. King James I granted a charter to the Virginia Company to colonize Virginia for profit. Three ships of colonizers left England on December 20, 1606, and landed in Virginia in April 1607. The company did not reveal who would be on the council that was to govern the colony until the ship reached Virginia. Once the ship landed, a sealed box was opened that listed seven council members, including the famous Captain John Smith. By May 1607, the settlers had established Jamestown as their colony.

Jamestown was to be self-sustaining with the colonists growing their own food. However, the colonists had trouble creating sustainable agriculture, hunting, and surviving through the winter. Further, supplies were hard to obtain from England. Smith took control and imposed strict discipline, requiring everyone to work. He also made friends with the local Powhatan Confederacy, which helped the colonists explore and provided them with important survival skills. When he returned to England in 1609, the colony fell into disarray. Only when the colony discovered and then began to grow tobacco and trade did it begin to thrive. This also proved that colonizing America was going to be a difficult affair that required a true commitment.

In 1702, the English East India Company merged with the "New" East India Company, whose charter is shown here. With this merger, the East India Company became the largest trading company in the world.

Separatists and colonists boarded the Mayflower *at Plymouth, England. The 180–ton ship held 102 passengers. The voyage took sixty–five days. Two people died during the long passage, and one child was born. The passengers chose the name Plymouth for the place where they finally landed in the New World.*

Religious Motivation

The other reason for colonization was the desire of individuals to have a better life. Some colonists wanted to move away from the overpopulated island of England. Others left for political or religious reasons. The Protestant Reformation began in 1517 when a Catholic priest named Martin Luther spoke out against certain practices of the Catholic Church. He wanted to change the church. When this did not happen, some people left the Catholic Church to form their own religious sects. This was a major cause of religious dissension.

In England, King Henry VIII had broken from the Roman Catholic Church in name. However, the beliefs and practices of the Church of England were still similar to those of the Catholic Church. Catholics were displaced and individuals who had different religious beliefs were often treated poorly. The New World was a possible safe haven to which many people who wished to practice their own religion without state interference fled.

A typical example of religious separatists who sought freedom in the New World was the Pilgrims. They held strict religious beliefs and were discriminated against in England. They first fled to the Netherlands and then thirty-five of them set sail on the *Mayflower* along with sixty-five other colonists. They landed at Plymouth, Massachusetts, in December 1620 and founded the Massachusetts Bay Colony. Before leaving the ship to found the colony, all members of the expedition signed the Mayflower Compact. This contract was a written agreement that established the idea of self-government.

While many separatists came to America looking for the freedom to practice their own religion, not all of them were willing to give such freedom to other groups. In fact, the Puritans in Massachusetts Bay mixed religion and government. This was sadly evident during the Salem witch trials, which started after two young girls began to act hysterically. A doctor claimed that they were bewitched, and others in the town also began to act strangely. People were accused of bewitching the girls and others. In the end, twenty people were executed, and another 150 were imprisoned before the governor stopped the trials completely.

Tituba's Confession ∽

Reverend Samuel Parris, who lived in Salem, Massachusetts, had brought a slave back from Barbados named Tituba. Betty Parris and three friends, including her cousin Abigail Williams, would often listen to stories told by Tituba about witchcraft and demons. The girls began acting strangely, and the village doctor claimed they were bewitched. Tituba was one of the first three people accused of practicing witchcraft. She confessed to practicing witchcraft and to signing a strange book owned by a man dressed in black. Tituba claimed that she had seen the names of the two other women who were accused of witchcraft in the same book, and all three were then put in jail.

Types of Colonies

The colonies that were set up by England fall into three major categories: charter, proprietary, and royal. Many of the colonies started as either charter or proprietary and became royal colonies as the times and the English rulers changed.

Charter colonies were established through legal charters given to private companies by the king. In other words, a company like the Virginia Company would be given the right to colonize a certain area. With this right came a great amount of freedom for the colony to control its own government and economy. This type of colony was often short-lived, as the crown would soon take back control. One of the most well-known charter colonies, Jamestown, only had its charter for seventeen years before becoming a royal colony.

On the other hand, the Massachusetts Bay Company was able to maintain control of Massachusetts throughout most of the 1600s. Other examples of charter colonies include Rhode Island, founded by Roger Williams, and Connecticut, founded by Thomas Hooker. Both of these men were Puritans who were dissatisfied with the Massachusetts Bay Colony and received charters for their own colonies from the crown.

A second type of colony that existed in the English colonial system was the proprietary colony. In this colony type, a single owner or small group of owners was granted the right to own a colony with privileges normally saved for the crown or official government. These owners were given the right to govern their new colonies. For example, King Charles II gave William Penn the right to found Pennsylvania. Penn not only founded the colony but was also its governor. Other examples of proprietary colonies included Georgia, North and South Carolina, Maryland, New York, and New Jersey. In the end, all of the proprietary colonies eventually became royal colonies,

Lady Rebecca ✏

According to legend, Pocahontas saved John Smith from being killed by her father, the Indian chief Powhatan. She and other members of her tribe helped the colonists at Jamestown in their quest to survive in the New World. She was later taken hostage by the colonists. She converted to Christianity, changed her name to Rebecca, and married John Rolfe, who was known as the first European to successfully grow and export tobacco. Lady Rebecca traveled to England with her husband. Sadly she contracted smallpox and died in England at the age of twenty-one. Many people today claim the Indian princess as an ancestor.

because the government wished to increase its power over the colonists as they moved toward open rebellion.

When a colony was ruled directly by the British government, this was called a royal colony. In this case, the government would appoint a royal governor who would represent the crown's interests in the colony. For example, Jamestown was founded through a charter to the Virginia Company. King James I revoked the company's charter in 1624 because there was a group of Puritans opposing him in Parliament that had also taken control of a large part of the Virginia Company. The company had also extended representative government to the colonists.

Virginia became a royal colony. King James I appointed Sir George Yeardley to be the governor of the colony. However, the roots of representative government were established in Virginia. From time to time the colonists were able to make gains in self-governance. Before the American Revolution almost all the colonies went through a period of royal control.

Nature of Colonial Governments

The thirteen American colonies were founded for different reasons and had unique governmental systems. The following is a look at each of the colonies, which will help give a sense of the differences between the history and outlook of each.

Virginia

Virginia began with the founding of Jamestown in 1607 through a charter to the Virginia Company. It became a royal colony in 1624 when that charter was revoked. However, before the charter was revoked, the first General Assembly met. This helped set a model for representative government in the colony. Many of the future leaders of the American Revolution would come from this colony including George Washington, Thomas Jefferson, James Madison, and James Monroe.

Maryland

Maryland was the first example of a proprietary government. George Calvert, the first Baron Baltimore, was a Catholic who lived in Protestant England. Catholics at that time were discriminated against, and Lord Baltimore asked for a charter to found a new colony in North America. This was granted after his death.

Lord Baltimore's son, Cecilius Calvert, the second Baron Baltimore, founded Maryland in 1634. The colony became known as a haven for Catholics. Lord Baltimore created a government in which he made the laws but only with the consent of the freemen who were landowners in the colony. In 1635, a legislative assembly met. Its role was to consent to the laws passed by the governor. The legislature would be divided into two houses with the freemen in one and the governor with his council in the other.

Massachusetts

Two colonies, Plymouth and Massachusetts Bay, combined to become Massachusetts by royal charter in 1691. Plymouth had been founded by Pilgrims in 1620 after receiving a land grant from the Virginia Company. They had formed their own government through a formal agreement called the Mayflower Compact.

On the other hand, the Massachusetts Bay Colony was created in 1630 by a group of merchants and Puritans who received a charter for their company from King Charles I. Because of an omission in their charter, the company was allowed to set up their own government without being ruled from England. The religious leader John Winthrop became governor of the colony. Power to rule the colony resided with the General Court of freemen who elected the governor and his assistants. Freemen had to be church members.

Wishing to keep more power for himself, Winthrop kept the terms of the charter given by King Charles I secret. It actually gave the freemen a greater amount of control and the power to levy taxes and pass laws. Winthrop and his assistants usurped that power until the town representatives demanded to see the charter in 1634. Once they

Cecilius Calvert was the second Baron Baltimore. Also referred to as Lord Baltimore, he was the founder and proprietary owner of the Maryland colony. While he never visited Maryland, his brothers Leonard and George headed the first expedition of colonists. Leonard was appointed governor of the new colony.

saw its terms, the General Court turned into a true representative legislative body. It was divided into two houses with the freemen in one, called the House of Deputies, and the governor and his assistants in the other, called the House of Assistants. Both houses had to agree in order to pass laws and increase taxes.

Rhode Island

The colony of Rhode Island was established by religious dissenters. Roger Williams was an outspoken Puritan who lived in the Massachusetts Bay Colony. He did not believe that the Puritan church and its leaders in Massachusetts Bay should have any dealings with the Anglican Church. He also believed that church and state should be completely separate so that no one would be forced to practice a religion if they did not want to. His beliefs were so radical that the General Court ordered him to return to England. Instead, aided by Narragansett (nar-uh-GAN-sit) Indians, Williams founded Providence, Rhode Island, in 1636.

Other religious dissenters like Anne Hutchinson also moved to and lived in Rhode Island. Williams was able to get a charter for his colony in 1643. This colony was founded on the ideas of a government based on the consent of the people, religious freedom, and the separation of church and state. It became a royal colony in 1663.

Connecticut

Connecticut was also founded by individuals who had broken off from the Massachusetts Bay Colony. In this case their goal was to find better lands. In 1637, Thomas Hooker helped organize the colony of Connecticut in order to have a means of common defense against the Pequot (PEE-kwat) Indians. A representative legislature similar to that of Massachusetts Bay was established called the

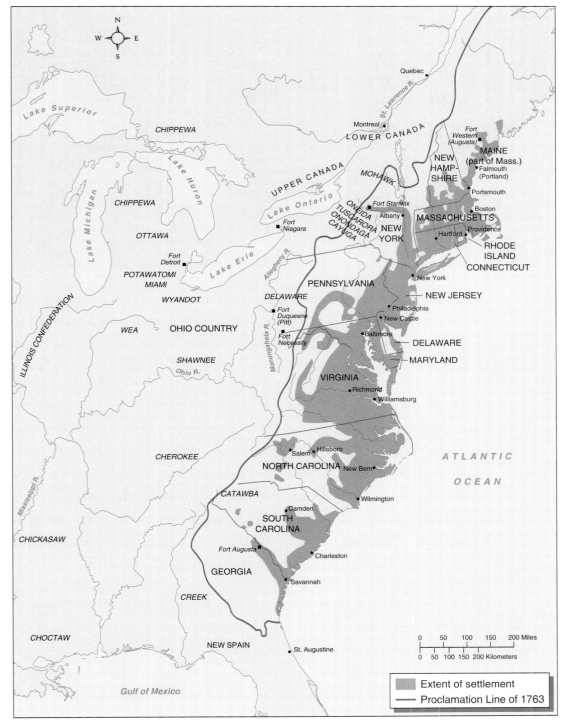

This map shows the holdings of the British in mainland North America by 1765. At this time, all thirteen colonies had been established. The approximate population of the colonies was over 1.2 million, with slaves making up one-fifth of that number. The colonies continued to expand westward into unsettled territory.

Extent of settlement

Proclamation Line of 1763

Thomas Hooker, pictured here preaching to a diverse crowd, was known to be a gifted preacher and a strong leader. This prominent Puritan helped found Connecticut because of his belief that all men of property should be allowed to vote regardless of their church membership. (This was not the case in Hooker's original colonial home of Massachusetts.) His leadership led to the passage of the Fundamental Orders of Connecticut.

General Court. In 1639, the legislature formally adopted the Fundamental Orders of Connecticut. These ensured that the government of the colony would be like that of Massachusetts. In 1662, Connecticut became a royal colony.

New Hampshire

New Hampshire was founded as a proprietary colony when the Council for New England gave a charter to Captain John Mason. Sir Ferdinando Gorges was also given lands that would later become Maine. Puritans from Massachusetts Bay helped settle the colony.

The government of New Hampshire consisted of a governor with his advisors and a representative assembly. Problems often arose between New Hampshire and Massachusetts Bay. For a time the two colonies were joined. Within New Hampshire those with religious interests often fought against those with economic interests for control of the government.

North Carolina

North and South Carolina started as one colony called Carolina in the 1660s when King Charles II awarded the land to eight lords proprietor. This proprietary colony was a reward to individuals who had remained loyal to the king while England had been in a state of civil war. The northern portion of the colony was somewhat neglected due to its geographic location. It was difficult for ships to find safe harbors. In fact, this portion of the colony consisted mostly of small settlements, with the first actual town not being founded until 1704. In 1719, South Carolina became a royal colony, separating it from its northern partner. The lords proprietor held onto North Carolina until 1729 when it too was deemed a royal colony.

South Carolina

Most of the settlements in the Carolinas were located in the southern part. Charles Town, which would become Charleston in 1783, was founded in 1670 by settlers who were given incentives by the lords proprietor. The government that was created through the Fundamental Constitutions of Carolina was complicated but favored large land ownership, which would eventually lead to the plantation system. The government also established religious freedom in the colony to attract settlers.

This partial list shows the huge land grants that the English provided to loyal subjects in the new colony of South Carolina. The first person on the list, Lady Margaret Yeamans, was the wife of the governor. Governor Yeamans had come to the colony from Barbados. He only served for four years in South Carolina before being replaced.

New York

New York was a proprietary colony based on a grant that King Charles II gave to his brother, the Duke of York and the future King James II, in 1664. James felt that New Amsterdam, which had been established by the Dutch, would be easy to seize, and this proved correct. He renamed the colony after his own title and called it New York. As the proprietor of the colony, he had the power to decide how the government would run.

James chose to give New York's citizens a limited form of self-government. He delegated ruling powers to a governor. The first governor was Richard Nicolls. By 1685, New York became a royal colony when James, now king, sent Sir Edmund Andros to be the royal governor. Andros ruled without a legislative body and caused much dissension among the colony's citizens.

New Jersey

After taking New Amsterdam, James gave the land between the Hudson and Delaware rivers to two loyal followers, Sir George Carteret and Lord John Berkeley. This territory was called Jersey and was divided in two parts, East and West Jersey. It was peopled by a wide variety of settlers including Puritans, Dutch, Swedes, Scots, Finns, and Quakers. In 1702, the east and west portions were combined when New Jersey was made a royal colony.

Pennsylvania

Pennsylvania was founded as a proprietary colony when William Penn was awarded a charter by King Charles II in 1681. Penn was a Quaker, a religious sect that did not believe in formal religious structure. The Quakers were extremely devout but saw religious experience as a personal endeavor. They did not believe in taking oaths, in recognizing ranks among people, or in fighting. Quakers recognized the equality of men and women and also would become important as abolitionists, opposing slavery.

Penn set up the colony of Pennsylvania as one of religious freedom. The government allowed for a representative legislature with popu-

larly elected government officials. Freemen who could vote included not only property holders but also taxpayers. The governor did not have the ability to veto laws passed by the assembly.

Delaware

In 1682, James, the Duke of York, gave Delaware to William Penn. Penn had argued that he needed the land to ensure the security of his own colony of Pennsylvania.

At first Pennsylvania and Delaware were joined, sharing the same legislative assembly. However, after 1701 Delaware was given the right to have its own assembly. Nevertheless, the governor of Pennsylvania was also the governor of Delaware. It was not until 1776 with

William Penn was known for his fair treatment of Native Americans. Here he is depicted completing a treaty with the Lenni Lenape Indians in November 1683. Penn was a firm believer in civil and religious liberties. His colonies became known for their tolerance of various Christian faiths.

The Quaker religion is a very individualized religion. In other words, there is no overriding religious "creed" for all Quakers, although many groups do have written statements of faith. Quaker meetings such as the one depicted here are noted for silence. Individuals speak only when the spirit moves them.

the Declaration of Independence that Delaware declared itself to be separate from Pennsylvania.

Georgia

Georgia was not established until 1732, only forty-four years before the Declaration of Independence was written. Therefore, it is no surprise that Georgia was not as involved in plans for independence in the beginning, since its connections were still very strong with England.

Georgia had been given to a group of twenty-one trustees by King George II. Its purpose was to serve as a buffer state between Spanish-held Florida and the other colonies. When General James Oglethorpe settled in Georgia at Savannah, the trustees created a colony whose goal was to establish a refuge for the poor and persecuted. As such, the colony did attract many people normally left out of society, including Protestants from central Europe, Scots, and Jews.

The government that was created was not effective, because many of the laws were not followed. For example, slavery was supposed to be illegal in order to help the poor get jobs. However, many people did not pay attention to this and slavery thrived.

In 1753, Georgia became a royal colony. The attempt to help the poor and persecuted had basically failed. Once the royal colony set up an effective government, the population grew steadily, and plantations growing rice and indigo became widespread.

Overall Differences

Despite some similarities, even at this early stage differences were developing between northern and southern colonies. The northern colonies, which had less land that was suitable for farming and a tougher climate, turned to making finished goods. The southern colonies, on the other hand, had an abundance of good land for farming. They also had the type of climate that allowed them to grow cash crops like tobacco and later cotton. The varying interests of the colonies would become important in later years as the fight for independence raged.

The thirteen colonies were founded for many different reasons. While their origins were diverse, their governments and laws laid the foundation for independence and government by the people. The colonies were often neglected by the crown for years at a time and left to grow and change on their own. They ruled themselves and established a very "American" way of government that stressed representative government and the separation of church and state.

The nineteenth–century artist Frederic Remington depicted the importance of trade and relations between the French and the Iroquois. Here a French explorer is talking to a council of Iroquois Indians. This council was part of the Iroquois Confederacy.

CHAPTER THREE ❧
Native American Tribes

WHEN CHRISTOPHER COLUMBUS made his fated first voyage and landed in the New World, he did not realize that he had found a land occupied by millions of Native Americans. North, Central, and South America were populated by numerous individual tribes or larger established societies. Archaeologists and anthropologists believe that these inhabitants had been living and thriving in the Americas for over 12,000 years.

Columbus thought he had landed in the Indies. Therefore, he and his men met people they called "Indians." He described them upon their first meeting as extremely generous and kind. He also noted, in a foreshadowing of future events, that they would be extremely easy to conquer. As he said, "with fifty men they could all be subjugated."

Columbus left the Americas to sail back to Europe, leaving behind a group of men. Upon his return, he found that in his absence the native population had been treated horribly by the Europeans. When the Indians attacked the Spanish because of this mistreatment, Columbus ordered an unequal response. He had whole villages slaughtered and captured 500 natives who were then sent to Europe as slaves. The Spanish crown was not in favor of his treatment of the native peoples. Columbus became more and more brutal and was eventually arrested for his actions against them.

Central American Civilizations

In Mexico and Peru, the Maya, Aztec, and Inca had established significant civilizations by the late fifteenth century. This was the time when the Spanish began exploring, subjugating, and colonizing the region. The Maya lived in much of Central America. They were highly advanced in terms of writing, mathematics, and astronomy, and in fact were the first society to use the number zero.

They built huge pyramids for religious and civic functions. However, their empire was large and did not have a strong central government to hold it together. For unknown reasons the Mayan culture fell apart around 900 C.E., possibly due to overpopulation, deforestation, and civil war. Their people were conquered by the Toltec whose governmental structure collapsed about 300 years later.

When the Spanish conquistador, Hernán Cortés, heard of the riches and the vast empire ruled by a man called Montezuma II, he set out to conquer Montezuma's people, the Aztec. Cortés burned the Spanish ships so that his men had no possibility of retreat. He also gained allies in several tribes who were paying taxes to Montezuma II.

The Aztec and Their Downfall

In 1325, the Aztec founded present-day Mexico City, which was called Tenochtitlán (teh-nohtch-tee-TLAN). This loosely organized society was ruled by warrior-priest elites who inherited their position at birth. The civilization was headed by an emperor. The society practiced human sacrifice as part of their religious rituals.

At the time when the Spanish invaded the Aztec Empire, there were over 5 million inhabitants. In 1519, Hernán Cortés and about 600 men landed in Mexico. With this small number, Cortés was able to take Tenochtitlán and eventually all of the Aztec Empire. Cortés was successful for many reasons. For one, he and his men not only had horses but also firearms with which to fight. Additionally, he was able to use deception to gain the trust of the Aztec emperor, Montezuma II. Cortés quickly

set himself up as the true ruler of Tenochtitlán with Montezuma II as a puppet emperor.

Many of the Aztec were unhappy with this situation and rebelled. Cortés was forced to leave, but he returned a year later to conquer the city again. He placed his officers in key roles overseeing the empire. Having disrupted and infiltrated the Aztec government, he and his men were able to conquer the entire Aztec civilization. Cortés and his men set up key landowners who were loyal to Spain. They were then able to keep the native population poor and subjugated. This helped Cortés consolidate his power and was a key step leading to the encomienda system, of large landholders with powers over the native peoples.

The Aztec Calendar 📎

The Aztec created a fascinating and complicated calendar. Similar to our present-day calendar it included a 365-day year. However, each month consisted of twenty days, with the last month being only five days long. The Aztec calendar also included a 260-day ritual cycle. Priests used the 260-day calendar to make predictions about the future.

Chichén Itzá was a great Mayan city that today is one of the most impressive archaeological sites in the world. Located in Mexico's Yucatán Peninsula, it shows the high level of advancement the Mayan people had achieved before European contact occurred. This picture is of El Caracol, a tenth–century Mayan observatory.

This map depicts the large number of Indian tribes present in North America in 1492. It is estimated that more than 5 million Native Americans lived north of the Rio Grande River at the time of their first meetings with the Europeans.

The Inca Empire and Its Downfall

The Inca Empire, located in the Andes Mountains in South America, was the largest civilization in America before the arrival of Columbus. It was well organized and connected by a series of roads. This system was ruled by a strong central government headed by the Sapa Inca. This emperor-like position was hereditary. Below the central government were four provinces, all of which met at the major city of Cuzco. Each province was ruled by a governor and local officials. Each family in the Inca Empire was required to give service to the government.

In 1533, Francisco Pizarro and a force of 180 soldiers and twenty-seven horses arrived in Cajamarca, where the last Incan emperor, Atahualpa (ah-tah-HWAL-pah) was, and demanded a meeting. When Atahualpa refused, Pizarro and his force of less than 200 men were able to successfully fight against the 80,000 Inca at the Battle of Cajamarca.

Pizarro captured Atahualpa and promised him freedom if he gathered a large amount of gold and silver. Atahualpa had the ransom collected, but Pizarro went ahead and had the emperor put to death for plotting against them. The Spanish finished the conquest of the Inca Empire in Peru when they took Cuzco in 1533 and were able to put down further rebellions. Pizarro created the capital of Peru in Lima as a central place from which to rule the colony.

English, French, and Dutch Relations

The English, French, and Dutch who settled in the northern part of North America also found a land populated by thousands of Indians. The French and the Dutch spent much of their time creating trading posts. They lived among the Native Americans in order to trade for fur. In general, their relationships with the native populations were cordial.

On the other hand, the English were more interested in creating permanent self-sustaining settlements. Therefore, it was not as necessary for them to work and cooperate with the Native American tribes. Relations between the English colonists and Native American tribes were often strained as the colonists would make treaties for land use and in many cases later break the terms of those treaties when they felt the need.

Organization of the Native Americans

Typically, the Native Americans of North America were not organized into complex civilizations like those of the Aztec, Inca, and Maya of Mexico and Central America. Instead, they were organized into tribes based upon ties of kinship. On a basic level, individual tribes often organized themselves based on a clan system. Clans were based on and connected by family ties. When individuals married from two different clans, their offspring would have rights and responsibilities in both clans. Groups of clans would then form a tribe.

Unlike many Western cultures, Native Americans often saw the fundamental unit of organization in their culture as based on social and family ties instead of geographic location, and they were often not organized based on their locality. However, many tribes still had defined geographic boundaries for their territory.

Some tribes were made up of hunters and gatherers while others were more established, with their people using farming to sustain themselves. Some tribes were independent states. Others attempted to create a higher level of organization by banding together through confederations. In the former case, all governmental controls lay in

the hands of the tribes themselves. Chiefs and headmen would meet periodically to create rules and laws for the tribe and pass judgment for any legal matters that might arise.

In many cases, independent tribes would ally with each other. This was generally on a temporary basis to deal with possible emergencies or common enemies. In fact, tribes would often fight between themselves over the right to specific territories. In these cases, the individual tribes were still independent, just as individual countries today that might ally with one another or fight are independent.

On the other hand, with confederations there was an overriding government. The goal of the confederation was to organize the tribes for common defense and legal structures. The individual

Trade was an important part of the interactions that occurred between Europeans and Native Americans. In fact, it was often the first form of contact between them. In the beginning, trade was beneficial for both sides, with the Europeans trading items such as guns and blankets in exchange for knowledge of the natives' farming techniques and tools, and for furs that were valuable back home.

tribes within the confederation were only responsible for governing their individual groups. These confederations were well organized and complex. A prime example of a confederation was the Iroquois Nation.

The Iroquois Nation

As the 1500s drew to a close, a well-developed confederation called the Iroquois Nation arose. This confederation was also known as the League of the Five Tribes of the Iroquois. The purpose of the confederation was multifold. The main reasons for its existence were to help maintain peace, security, and justice, and to create a common law. The alliance was very strong, and the Dutch and English had to work with it in order to continue to trade for furs.

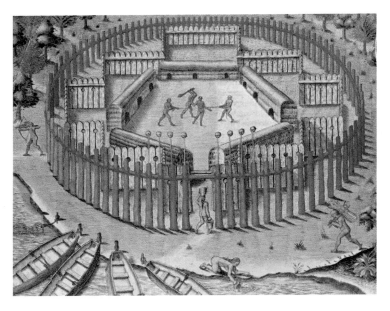

This etching, from the 1580s, was based on a first-hand account of a Native American village. You can see how the villagers surrounded the settlement with poles stuck in the ground. This provided at least some fortification against attacks.

The Iroquois Nation consisted of over 12,000 members. They were governed by fifty sachems (SA-chums), or governing leaders, who made decisions for all the villages. Women were given the power to control the nominations for tribal councils. As the members of the Iroquois Nation traded with the European colonists, they received firearms. They then used these as they went to war with neighboring tribes. Eventually, the fierce warriors of the Iroquois Nation were able to gain control of large areas of the eastern half of North America. This incursion against other tribes led to a war against the French and their Indian allies in the 1690s. After this war, the Iroquois made

This map of North America in 1600 shows the locations of the native peoples and the extent of the Spanish presence in present-day Florida, Mexico, Central America, and the Caribbean.

The Pequot War was the first major armed conflict between the Native Americans and the English settlers in New England. Almost all the Pequot Indians were killed in this war. When it officially ended in September 1683, the few remaining survivors signed the Tripartite Treaty, which officially dissolved their tribe.

peace with the French and were able to stay neutral between France and Great Britain until the French and Indian War began in 1754.

Native Americans and Colonists

When Europeans arrived in North and Central America, they disrupted the way of life of many of the native population. Even those colonists who tried to live in harmony with neighboring tribes had an effect on the environment. Further, as previously stated, Europeans often spread diseases for which the native population had no defenses.

Native Americans treated the colonists in varying ways. Many were at first cautiously helpful, for example helping the settlers at

Cooperation and Conflict ❧

Relations between Native Americans and colonists went through periods of cooperation and conflict depending on many factors. From the beginning, colonists took over land that had once been occupied by Native American tribes. They spread disease that had been unknown and caused problems for the Indians. At the same time, however, they brought the native population technological advances such as better cooking tools and weapons. A prime example of cooperation was what has been called the "First Thanksgiving," even though it was not repeated. Pilgrims at Plymouth held a three-day feast shared with ninety Indians. This happened in 1621. On the other hand, the first major Indian uprising occurred in Jamestown in 1622 and resulted in the deaths of 347 colonists.

Jamestown survive their first winter. However, over time the cultural differences became too much. Colonists continued to take over more and more traditionally tribal lands. This eventually led to many conflicts between the native peoples and the colonists.

One example was the Pequot War of 1637. The Pequot Indians attacked Puritans in Massachusetts and Connecticut. This attack was in revenge for a raid that had been made against a Pequot village where everyone had been killed. In the fighting that followed, the colonists were aided by the Narragansett Indians. They killed many Pequot Indians and sold the rest into slavery.

In 1638, the Pequot nation was dissolved, which resulted in a temporary peace that ended in 1676 with King Philip's War. In the end, many Native American tribes could not reconcile their way of life with that of the colonists, especially the English ones.

This engraving is titled "Introduction to Slavery." It shows a slave being presented to a group of men. He and the other slaves in the background have been brought off the ship, pictured in the background, to be sold into slavery.

CHAPTER FOUR ∂
Government Structures

FOUR NATIONS VIED FOR TERRITORY AND created working societies in the "new world" of North, Central, and South America: France, Spain, England, and the Netherlands. Of those four, only England created lasting colonies that were allowed to rule themselves. France and Spain were more concerned with keeping order and making profits. They ruled their territories from afar using crown-appointed authorities. The colonists themselves did not spend much time ruling themselves. With the Netherlands, companies looking for profit worked to organize and rule the territories, again without the colonists being allowed to self-rule. The English colonies, on the other hand, were given ample opportunity to create their own governmental structures and rule themselves. This was due to many reasons, not the least of which was that issues back in England distracted the crown and Parliament from ruling the colonies too closely.

When the English began settling America, they brought three specific ideas that helped shape the government that would eventually become the government of the United States. The first of these ideas was that government should be limited in its power. Second, they believed that government should be representative, allowing those being governed to have a say. Finally, government should be well ordered. Local ruling bodies should create the laws for towns and smaller areas. The larger central government would create colony-wide laws. These ideas were very important for the development of governments in the individual colonies and eventually for the call for independence.

Magna Carta

The English arrived with these notions of government based on events and documents in England's history. One document that is pointed to as central in the history of English law was the Magna Carta, which means Great Charter. In 1215, a group of English nobles forced King John to sign the Magna Carta. This document allowed for the right to a trial by jury. It also required the due process of law so that the crown could not take away someone's life without cause. Of course at that time the document only applied to the nobles. Nonetheless, these protections meant that the power of the king would no longer be absolute. No longer could he claim complete authority.

Parliament

Parliament was the legislative body in England at the time when the English were first settling America. It consisted of two houses: a House of Lords, in which membership was hereditary, and a House of Commons, to which representatives were elected.

The idea of a legislative body that worked with the king originally arose from the idea of a King's Council. After William the Conqueror invaded Britain in 1066, he created the Curia Regis or King's Council. This group advised the king on domestic and foreign affairs. However, this body was chosen by the king and was not representative of the people.

The first elected Parliament was called in 1265 for the purpose of agreeing to proposed taxes. By 1295, King Edward I called for the second "Model Parliament," again with elected representatives and hereditary lords meeting to help approve taxes. This was the beginning of the idea of representative government in England. During this period the king still had most of the power.

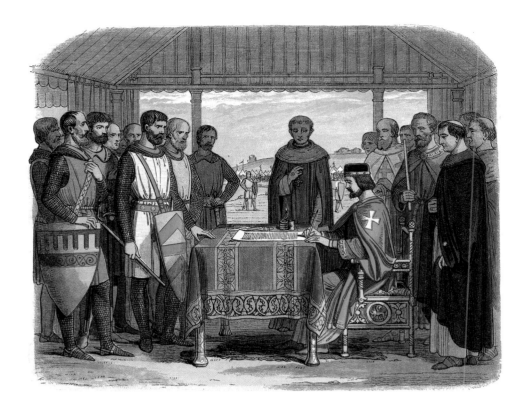

King John of England, seated to the right, is being forced to sign the Magna Carta in 1215. He met the nobles in tents set up on the meads, or meadows, at Runnymede to negotiate the clauses that would be included in the document. They chose a large, open area, because the number of people involved in the negotiations was enormous.

Over the years, Parliament and the king increasingly clashed as the two houses decided to assert more power. In 1628 Parliament would not agree to raise taxes unless King Charles I signed the Petition of Right. Similar to the Magna Carta, the Petition of Right reinforced the idea that the king was limited in his power and must obey laws just like other English citizens. Then in 1688, the Bill of Rights was passed, which further decreased the power of the monarchy and increased rights for citizens.

Mayflower Compact

The ideas of self-rule through representative government began with the first major settlements in America. When the settlers on the *Mayflower* arrived at Plymouth, Massachusetts, in 1620, they, as a group, agreed to the Mayflower Compact. This important document was the first written agreement for mutual government in the New World. It was signed by forty-one of the 102 passengers on the *Mayflower*. The text of the Mayflower Compact follows:

The Compact

Signed in the Cabin of the "Mayflower," Nov. 11th, Old Style, Nov. 21st, New Style, 1620.

"In the name of God, amen, we whose names are underwritten, the loyall subjects of our dread soveraigne Lord, King James, by the grace of God, of Great Britaine, Franc and Ireland king, defender of the faith, &c., haveing undertaken, for the glorie of God, and advancement of the Christian faith, and honor of our king and countrie, a voyage to plant the first colonie in the northerne parts of Virginia, doe by these presents solemnly and mutualy in the presence of God, and one of another, covenant and combine ourselves together into a civill body politick, for our better ordering and preservation and furtherance of the ends aforesaid; and by vertue hereof to enacte, constitute and frame such just and equall laws, ordenances, acts, constitutions and offices, from time to time, as shall be thought most meete and convenient for the general good of the colonie, unto which we promise all due submission and obedience. In witness whereof we have hereunto subscribed our names at Cap-Codd the 11 of November, in the year of the raigne of our soveraigne lord, King James of England, Franc and Ireland the eighteenth, and of Scotland the fifty-fourth, ANo Dom 1620."

JOHN CARVER.
WILLIAM BRADFORD.
EDWARD WINSLOW.
WILLIAM BREWSTER.
ISAAC ALLERTON.
MYLES STANDISH.
JOHN ALDEN.
SAMUEL FULLER.
CHRISTOPHER MARTIN.
WILLIAM MULLINS.
WILLIAM WHITE.
RICHARD WARREN.
JOHN HOWLAND.
STEPHEN HOPKINS.
EDWARD TILLY.
JOHN TILLY.
FRANCIS COOKE.
THOMAS ROGERS.
THOMAS TINKER.
JOHN RIDGDALE.
EDWARD FULLER.
JOHN TURNER.
FRANCIS EATON.
JAMES CHILTON.
JOHN CRACKSTON.
JOHN BILLINGTON.
MOSES FLETCHER.
JOHN GOODMAN.
DIGORY PRIEST.
THOMAS WILLIAMS.
GILBERT WINSLOW.
EDMOND MARGESON.
PETER BROWN.
RICHARD BRITTERIDGE.
GEORGE SOULE.
RICHARD CLARKE.
RICHARD GARDINER.
JOHN ALLERTON.
THOMAS ENGLISH.
EDWARD DOTY.
EDWARD LISTER.

This paper was made by hand in 1898.

A. S. BURBANK, Publisher, Pilgrim Bookstore, Plymouth, Mass.

The original Mayflower Compact has never been found, although many copies were made and distributed. The Pilgrims who signed the Mayflower Compact elected John Carver to be their governor.

In the name of God, Amen. We, whose names are underwritten, the Loyal Subjects of our dread Sovereign Lord, King James, by the Grace of God, of England, France and Ireland, King, Defender of the Faith, e&. Having undertaken for the Glory of God, and Advancement of the Christian Faith, and the Honour of our King and Country, a voyage to plant the first Colony in the northern Parts of Virginia; Do by these Presents, solemnly and mutually, in the Presence of God and one another, covenant and combine ourselves together into a civil Body Politick, for our better Ordering and Preservation, and Furtherance of the Ends aforesaid; And by Virtue hereof to enact, constitute, and frame, such just and equal Laws, Ordinances, Acts, Constitutions and Offices, from time to time, as shall be thought most meet and convenient for the general Good of the Colony; unto which we promise all due Submission and Obedience. In Witness whereof we have hereunto subscribed our names at Cape-Cod the eleventh of November, in the Reign of our Sovereign Lord King James, of England, France, and Ireland, the eighteenth, and of Scotland the fifty-fourth, Anno Domini, 1620.

This document was significant because it relied on the idea of a social contract. This was the belief that the people had the duty to follow the government as long as it protected them and their basic rights. If the government failed to do this, then the people could dissolve it. By signing the Mayflower Compact, the settlers were agreeing to follow the rules of the government. At the same time, they expected the government to look out for the best interests of the people. In other words, the government was made legitimate with the consent of the people who signed the compact.

The individuals aboard the *Mayflower* consisted of many Pilgrims, including those who wished to break away from the Church of England. The settlers formed the Plymouth Colony. Despite their best efforts, after the first winter almost half of them had died. In 1621, William Bradford became the governor and was able to form a friendship with Massasoit (MAS-uh-soit), the leader of the Wampanoag Indians, who helped teach the settlers ways to survive in America.

Jamestown and the Rise of the House of Burgesses

Jamestown had been founded in 1607 by the Virginia Company. However, within the next ten years it was failing miserably. Those in charge of the Virginia Company decided to make some changes. These were meant to help attract more people to Jamestown. They also hoped the changes would increase the productivity and happiness of those already settled there. They promised fifty acres of land to anyone who could find passage to Virginia. They also began to relax some of their rules for colonists.

One extremely important reform they made was that the colony was going to follow English Common Law as the basis for its legal system. In other words, colonists would have the rights of "Englishmen." This was a definite improvement from the power held by the appointed governor. Even more important than that, however, was the creation of the House of Burgesses. This was the first assembly of colonists in the New World. It allowed them to have a voice in the local government.

The first General Assembly of Virginia met in July 1619 in Jamestown. In the beginning, the body represented the interests of the governor, his personal council, and the owners of the largest plantations. The latter were called the burgesses and were elected by land-owning males who were over seventeen.

The role of the House of Burgesses was to make laws for the colony. However, the governor, his council, and even the Virginia Company's directors in London could veto the laws. When Virginia reverted to a royal colony in 1624, the House of Burgesses continued to meet, but their power was reduced. This first governmental body would continue to grow in its importance in the development of independence in the future.

Fundamental Orders of Connecticut

In 1638, three Connecticut towns chose representatives who met to create a new constitution. Reverend Thomas Hooker gave a sermon at the opening session in which he espoused his view that "the foundation of authority is laid in the free consent of the people." The constitution that was adopted in 1639 was called the Fundamental Orders of Connecticut.

The Fundamental Orders of Connecticut vested all power to rule in the people themselves instead of in a higher power, including either God or a government outside of Connecticut. The constitution was important for creating the first such government of the people. In its opening it said,

> . . . the Inhabitants and Residents of Windsor, Hartford and Wethersfield are now cohabiting and dwelling in and upon the River of Connectecotte and the lands thereunto adjoining; and well knowing where a people are gathered together the word of God requires that to maintain the peace and union of such a people there should be an orderly

and decent Government . . . do therefore associate and conjoin our-selves to be as one Public State or Commonwealth. . . .

According to the constitution, the general assembly would meet twice a year. The governor would be chosen for one year from the representatives along with six other magistrates to administer the law. There was even a provision in the constitution for collecting taxes from among the towns. Eventually, the basic idea behind the U.S. Constitution would derive in part from these Fundamental Orders.

Religious Freedom

One significant foundation of many colonial governments was that of religious freedom. Many people came to America searching for such freedom. Often they had faced persecution for their religious beliefs in their home countries. They had come from lands where the government had set a state religion. Even though in England it might not have been illegal to espouse a religion other than the Church of England, different sects were still discriminated against. Colonists wanted to be able to choose their own religion and worship without fear of persecution.

The Puritans and later the Quakers would form their own colonies based on their beliefs. The Puritans actually wished to keep their colony free for their Puritan beliefs but not necessarily for other sects. They persecuted those who did not conform to their ways and their government was intertwined with their religious beliefs.

Roger Williams did not believe that the Puritan leaders in Massachusetts Bay were being strict enough in their religious beliefs. He led a group of settlers away to form a new colony that would become

The Charter Oak was a white oak tree that served as the hiding place for the charter of Connecticut so that Sir Edmund Andros, a representative of King James II, could not find and revoke it. When the great tree fell during a storm in 1856, it was deemed to have been about 1,000 years old. The Charter Oak is commemorated on the Connecticut state quarter released in 1999.

Anabaptists, or rebaptizers, were part of the Protestant Reformation. They believed that only those who could consciously accept Jesus Christ as their personal savior should be baptized, and thus infant baptism was not valid. Further, they believed that only biblical scriptures should form the basis of Christian faith.

Rhode Island. Despite his stricter beliefs, he was a staunch defender of the idea of the separation of church and state. He felt that it was terrible for individuals to be forced to worship against their own beliefs. Rhode Island was founded on this principle.

Pennsylvania was founded by the Quaker William Penn, based on the idea of religious freedom. Individuals from other religious sects were welcome to live in the state and were not persecuted for their beliefs. Maryland became a haven for Catholics who were persecuted in England and by many New World Protestants.

In the end, America became a land of many religions. As the population increased, more and more sects arrived. With the increase in the number of different religious sects came a decrease in religious persecution. In 1649, the Act Concerning Religion, also known as the Maryland Toleration Act, was enacted. This was considered an important step toward religious freedom in America although it did not extend beyond the Christian religions. In part, it stated:

> [N]o person or persons whatsoever within this Province, or the islands, ports, harbors, creekes, or havens thereunto belonging professing to believe in Jesus Christ, shall from henceforth be any waies troubled, molested or discountenanced for or in respect of his or her religion nor in the free exercise thereof within this Province or the islands thereunto belonging nor any way compelled to the beleif or exercise of any other Religion against his or her consent. . . .

Religion was extremely important throughout the American colonies. Eventually religious freedom would be included as part of the First Amendment to the U.S. Constitution. At that point the separation of church and state in the United States would be complete.

New England Town Meetings

An important move toward democracy in the colonies occurred with the New England town meetings. These were the only examples of direct democracy institutions in the United States whereby assembled voters would actually make the laws. This form of direct democracy had been practiced in Greece in the fifth century B.C.E. but was very rare. In fact, the European countries that had settled America all had one form or another of monarchy. This meant that the majority of power lay with the king. In England the monarchy was limited by the power of Parliament, but democracy still did not exist.

In a New England town meeting, the date and time of the meeting would be posted along with the scheduled agenda. All eligible voters were allowed to attend, although this does not mean that they all actually participated. Further, the eligible voters often included only the male landowners. Nevertheless, this idea of the voters being able to have a say in local politics was a significant event in American governmental history.

The eventual system that the United States adopted was not one of pure direct democracy, which would have been unmanageable and actually impossible, but instead one of representative democracy. With representative democracy, all the people get to vote for their representatives who then represent their interests in Congress.

Undemocratic Features of the Colonies

These colonial governments, despite the advances that were being made with them, still had many undemocratic features. For example, most colonies only allowed individuals who owned property to participate in the government and vote. If a person did not own any land, he was not allowed to vote. By the 1750s, the amount of property required made it possible for most adult males to vote once they reached their thirties. However, only white males would be considered eligible for voting rights.

In most colonies, those who could vote for the office could serve in the legislature. However, in South Carolina, Georgia, New Jersey, and New Hampshire, males had to have a significant number of acres to be able to hold political office. Since officeholders were not paid for their time, most of those who were elected, and were therefore making the laws, were wealthy.

Many settlers who arrived from Europe and, at first, from Africa came as indentured servants. This meant that they had to work for a set number of years to pay off the price of their passage before they would be given the freedom to settle on their own. Until the indentured servants paid off their debts, they were unable to leave their employer and would be considered fugitives if they ran away. Indentured servitude would continue past the founding of the United States. In fact, Andrew Johnson, the seventeenth president of the United States, was bound as an indentured servant to a tailor before he escaped and set up his own shop.

In 1619, Africans arrived at Jamestown as indentured servants to work with the settlers. However, the ability of Africans to work as indentured servants was quickly taken away with the creation of the Royal African Company in 1672. This company transported Africans to the colonies as slaves. Over time, many colonies in the North outlawed slavery. However, this terrible enterprise would continue in the middle and southern colonies until the American Civil War, almost 100 years after the founding of the United States.

Colonial governments typically treated slaves as property. As property, slaves could not own property, enter contracts, or vote. The governments also treated women as the lesser sex, a group to be protected. The way women were viewed politically was not that different from the way slaves in many colonies were seen. The difference was in the reason behind the laws that were enacted. Women were to be protected from voting and public life, while slaves, because they were property, did not deserve the same rights as white men.

Women married young and in most cases once married were not allowed to own property in

their own right. Only when they were widowed were they given more of a right to financial freedom. They were not able to participate in the government or vote for political office.

Native Americans were not included in colonial American political life. They were not seen as citizens of the colonies and instead were treated as foreign groups. Colonial governments created treaties with many Indian tribes for lands and trading rights. However, individual Indians were not afforded any rights within colonial governments.

Despite the mistreatment of various groups in colonial America, the seeds were being planted for freedoms and liberties that would eventually extend to all citizens. The idea that government was there to protect the people, that citizens should have a say, and that royal authority should be limited were central to the future of America. By the end of the colonial period, the colonial assemblies had taken a great amount of political power away from the colonial governor and his personal council.

Tobacco was an important crop for early settlers in Jamestown. John Rolfe is credited with crossbreeding the indigenous tobacco of the area with some from the Caribbean to create a tobacco that was easy to grow and considered pleasant to smoke. This cash crop was easily sold in England and led to the tremendous growth of the colony.

British regiments were made up mostly of infantry. The "Redcoats" typically carried a flintlock musket with a long bayonet attached. Because of the limitations of flintlock muskets, which could at best fire three shots in a minute, battles were typically staged with musket fire and then a charge forward that allowed the soldiers to use their bayonets.

CHAPTER FIVE ❧
The Developing Colonies

EACH OF THE COLONIES DEVELOPED SEPARATELY. While they were located on the same continent, they did not have much reason to work together. Each had its own history and government. However, over time the colonies found that there were occasions when it was necessary for them to work together. Visionaries like Benjamin Franklin attempted to unify the colonies years before the fight for independence began.

New England Confederation

In 1637, New England colonists fought their first major armed conflict against a Native American tribe in the Pequot War. The Massachusetts Bay and Plymouth colonies joined together with the Narragansett and Mohegan Indians to fight against the Pequot. As a result of this war, leaders from the New England colonies agreed to meet. Their goal was to create a plan for mutual defense against future attacks by Native Americans.

Delegates from Connecticut, New Haven, Massachusetts Bay, and Plymouth met in 1643 in Boston, Massachusetts. The meeting did not include Maine or Rhode Island. The group formed the New England Confederation, which included two delegates from each of the colonies. The Confederation was to hold annual meetings and required three-quarters of all the delegates to agree to any measures.

It was not the goal of the confederation to create a central government for the colonies. Instead, they were trying to protect themselves through their alliance. The confederation, however, did require each of the colonies to pay for mutual defense. It also included an agreement to return fugitives and runaway slaves to member colonies.

The confederation did not have an effective way to enforce its decisions. Massachusetts was the largest of the colonies involved in the confederation. Because of its size, it was able to ignore decisions with which it did not agree. No other members could force Massachusetts to follow the confederation's decision. For example, it ignored the decision to protect Connecticut during the Anglo-Dutch conflict in the 1650s.

English Civil War and Restoration

King Charles II of England reigned from 1660 to 1685. During his time as king, the city of New Amsterdam was seized and later renamed New York. Charles II also granted charters for the foundation of the Carolina, New Jersey, and Pennsylvania colonies. Charles II secretly became a Catholic in 1670, even though the majority of Parliament was Protestant at the time.

England experienced a civil war beginning in 1642. It lasted until 1649 when King Charles I was deposed and beheaded. Oliver Cromwell then set up the Puritan Commonwealth and Protectorate, which ruled in England until 1660. At that point King Charles II was restored to the throne. This event is called the Restoration. During the years of its civil war, England did not pay attention to the colonies. Shipments ceased and communications lagged. Therefore, the New England colonies especially enjoyed a period of more intense self-rule.

Once the Restoration occurred, England once again set its eyes on the colonies. The goal was to increase England's control and the monetary rewards it expected from its colonies. To gain greater control, England began passing laws to ensure that it, and not other nations, benefited from imports and exports from the colonies. Cromwell had attempted to take back control by passing the Navigation Act of

1651. This stated that all goods imported to England or the colonies must be transported on English ships.

In 1660, King Charles II had another navigation act passed that included a list of "enumerated goods" that could only be sold to England. These included important crops such as tobacco, cotton, and sugar. Three years later England increased its control by adding that all items must be sold to England. The English merchants could then sell them again for greater profit. Finally, in 1673 an act was passed that required that a tax be paid on all enumerated goods.

In order to ensure that the colonies followed these increasingly drastic trade measures, King Charles II created the Lords of Trade. This group created colonial governors and sent tax collectors to the colonies. Massachusetts Bay Colony lost its charter when it failed to follow the laws.

Dominion of New England

After Charles II died in 1685, his brother James II became king. He went further to enforce the laws by dissolving all colonial governments and creating the Dominion of New England. The government was to be run by a royal governor named Sir Edmund Andros, who ruled from Boston, Massachusetts. The governor and his council were to rule without colonial representation. Andros imprisoned those who fought against the laws and did not allow town governments to meet.

In 1688, King James II was deposed in favor of his Protestant daughter, Mary, and her Dutch husband, William of Orange. This was called the Glorious Revolution. Andros was arrested in Boston and all of the colonies reverted to their former forms of government. The assemblies were from then on more of a part of each colony's administration. These events were extremely important in creating a growing sense of unhappiness with the crown. With the Glorious Revolution came new laws in England, including the Bill of Rights and the Toleration Act, that ensured increased rights for citizens and religious freedom.

The overthrow of the monarch led people to realize that government could be limited and citizens had the right to overthrow it if necessary. John Locke wrote his famous *Two Treatises of Government* based on these events. In it he explained that people had the God-given right to life, liberty, and property. The government was seen as a contract between the leaders and the people. If the government failed on its end, then the people had the right to rise up and revolt.

William and Mary did not repeal the Navigation Acts but instead worked to enforce them more efficiently. In 1696, Britain created the Lords Commissioners of Trade and Plantations, also called the Board of Trade, which monitored commerce and helped plan colonial policy. However, once George I ascended the throne in 1714, the power of the royal government once again waned in the colonies.

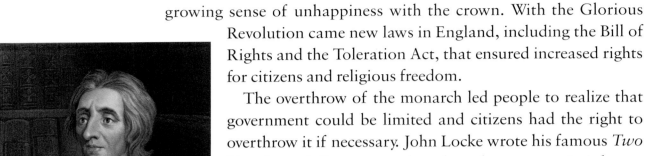

John Locke was not only an English philosopher but also a physician and an economist. He wrote several significant works, including many on toleration and the importance of the separation of church and state.

Zenger Trial

Other freedoms that are important to the United States today also arose during the colonial period. Freedom of the press to report on the events of the government without interference is an important right. A significant event on the path to freedom of the press was the Zenger trial that occurred on August 5, 1735.

John Peter Zenger, a German immigrant, was charged with printing "seditious libels" (in English Common Law, written words that are intended to spread hatred or discontent against the government) in the *New York Weekly Journal*. However, despite the royal governor's desire to have Zenger found guilty, the jury of twelve found him not guilty. This decision was mainly because Zenger's writings were based on fact and not made up with intent to harm. This decision was an important step toward allowing a free press, a necessary part of a free society.

French and Indian War

The French and Indian War, which lasted from 1754 until 1763, was a turning point in colonial American history for many reasons. This conflict was a war fought on two fronts: Europe and North America. It began in North America and was named the French and Indian

Join or Die ✑

During the French and Indian War, Benjamin Franklin published what became the first political cartoon published in an American newspaper. Published in the *Pennsylvania Gazette* on May 9, 1754, it pictured a snake cut into eight sections, representing the colonies. New England was the head of the snake and South

Carolina was its tail. Under the snake was written "JOIN, or DIE." The cartoon alluded to the idea that the colonies must unify in order to defeat the French. The cartoon became popular during the Revolutionary War and again during the American Civil War.

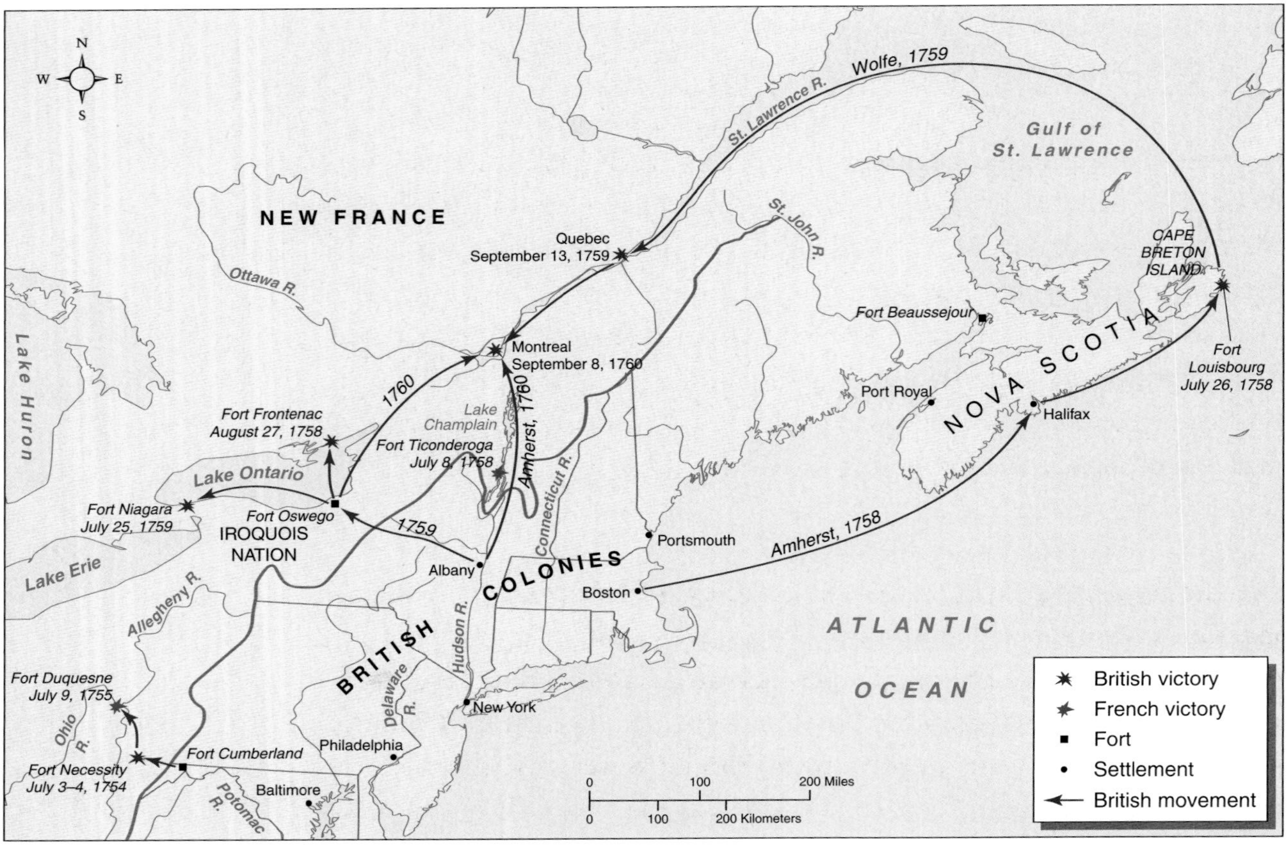
N
S
E
W
NEW FRANCE
Wolfe, 1759
St. Lawrence R.
Gulf of St. Lawrence
St. John R.
Quebec September 13, 1759
CAPE BRETON ISLAND
Ottawa R.
Lake Huron
Fort Beausséjour
Montreal September 8, 1760
Fort Louisbourg July 26, 1758
1760
Port Royal
NOVA SCOTIA
Fort Frontenac August 27, 1758
Lake Champlain
Halifax
Fort Ticonderoga July 8, 1758
Amherst, 1760
Connecticut R.
Lake Ontario
Fort Niagara July 25, 1759
Fort Oswego
1759
IROQUOIS NATION
Portsmouth
Amherst, 1758
Lake Erie
Albany
COLONIES
Allegheny R.
Boston
BRITISH
Hudson R.
ATLANTIC
OCEAN
Delaware R.
Fort Duquesne July 9, 1755
New York
Ohio R.
Fort Cumberland
Philadelphia
Fort Necessity July 3–4, 1754
Potomac R.
Baltimore
0 100 200 Miles
0 100 200 Kilometers
British victory
French victory
Fort
Settlement
British movement

This map depicts the major events of the French and Indian War, which lasted from 1754 to 1763. Under the treaty that ended the war, Great Britain owned all land east of the Mississippi River, excluding New Orleans. Even though the war was over, conflicts still occurred on the western frontier between British colonists and Native Americans until 1764.

War because the French allied with Native Americans of the Ohio Valley to fight the British. When the war spread to Europe, it became known as the Seven Years War. The fight was over who would dominate colonial endeavors and world trade.

The French and English had been living fairly peacefully together on the North American continent. However, over time problems began to arise over religion, trade, and territory. In 1749, British colonists received a huge grant of land from the British crown in the Ohio Valley, a land that had already been claimed for France. Wishing to stop the British from expanding into their territory, the French began building forts. The English in turn also began building their own forts and building up their military.

In 1754, the conflict came to a head when George Washington,

George Washington: British Soldier ❧

George Washington held a commission in the British army. In April 1754, Washington led a group of soldiers to help the British in their bid for land in the Ohio Valley. During that campaign, he decided to investigate what a group of French soldiers were doing near his position. When he and his troops arrived at the French campsite, someone fired a shot, which led to a skirmish that killed ten Frenchmen, including an officer. The French claimed they were attacked without cause by Washington and his men. This skirmish was the first armed conflict in what would eventually become the French and Indian War.

then a colonel, was sent to the Ohio Valley to thwart the French expansion. Overall, his mission was not a success, although it did build Fort Necessity in the region. The French attacked this new fort, forcing Washington to surrender. At this point, the French and Indian War officially began. It was not until 1756, however, that the conflict spread to Europe.

At first, the British were losing. When William Pitt, British secretary of state, attempted to force the colonists to help with the war effort, he was met with great resistance. Only after he moved away from forcing their involvement and instead began sending troops from England did the colonists fully support the war. In the end, the British won and the French gave up claims to any lands east of the Mississippi River.

Albany Plan of Union

An important result of the French and Indian War was that it was the first time individuals from different colonies united to fight a common enemy. In fact, the British themselves started this when they called the Albany Conference.

Chief Pontiac was able to gather together and become the head of an intertribal group called the Council of Three Tribes. He organized local tribes to attack British forts in the Ohio Territory during May 1762. The tribes briefly captured eight of the forts before being defeated by the British.

The Albany Conference was the meeting of a group of official delegates from six colonies, including Connecticut, Maryland, Massachusetts, New Hampshire, Pennsylvania, and Rhode Island, and one unofficial delegate from New York. They met in Albany, New York, from June 19 to July 11, 1754, at the request of British officials. The goals of the conference were twofold. First, the delegates were to find a better way of dealing with the Native American tribes. Their second goal was to come up with common defenses against the French in the French and Indian War that had recently begun.

Representatives from the Iroquois Confederacy met at the conference with the delegates and created a treaty. However, it did not last long. In fact, many members of the Iroquois Confederacy ended up fighting with the French against the British in the French and Indian War.

An important event at the Albany Conference was the proposal by Benjamin Franklin to create a union of the colonies. This was called the Albany Plan of Union. This plan was to go beyond the original intention of the conference. It would have created a colonial government over all the existing colonies except Delaware and Georgia. The plan passed unanimously at the conference but was rejected by both the individual colonial legislatures and by King George II.

The Albany Plan included having a president-general, appointed by the king, along with a grand council. This was a legislature with representatives from each colony. The plan was the first official attempt to create a unified colonial government. Parts of it were actually used in the Articles of Confederation and the Constitution. Ironically, if the king and the colonies had accepted the Albany Plan, the Revolutionary War might not have occurred when it did. As Benjamin Franklin would state in 1789, the plan would have allowed the colonies as a whole to provide their own defense. Therefore the British would not have had to post a standing army in the colonies after the French and Indian War.

Results of the French and Indian War

The major result from the French and Indian War was an increasing desire on the part of the British to take greater control over the colonies. There was resentment on the part of many British military and governmental leaders. They felt that while they were overseas to protect the colonists, they did not receive the level of monetary or

Fort Necessity was a small, hastily built stockade located in Pennsylvania. George Washington oversaw the building of the stockade, which took five days. Washington's surrender at this fort was the only time in his career that he was forced to surrender. The French burned the fort before returning to their own Fort Duquesne.

military support that they expected from the colonists. Once the "Redcoats," or British soldiers, so named because of the color of their uniform, were in North America, the British decided to have them stay for "protection." The British felt the need to take greater control over the colonies and in many instances reorganize the government to give the mother country more control.

With the Treaty of Paris, signed in 1763, officially ending the French and Indian War, the British gained many lands once owned by France. In fact, they controlled all the land east of the Mississippi River. Settlers wanted to move into the newly acquired Ohio Valley now that the French were gone. However, the land was owned by the Indian nations. In 1763, Pontiac's Rebellion began along the frontier.

The Ohio Valley Indians had been allies of the French and were upset when they were told that they now had to be loyal to the British. Pontiac, a leader of the Ottawa Indians, argued for a return to traditional ways and a rejection of the British. He gained allies among many other Native American tribes in the area. They attacked and laid siege to various forts, eight of which fell to the tribes. Eventually, two different British armies were able to win and make peace with the allied tribes. One result of the war was that the British passed the Proclamation of 1763. This did not allow any settlements west of the Allegheny Mountains, and it also created new governing structures in four areas of the territory gained from the war.

The stated reason for this was to keep the colonists safe while helping calm fears on the part of the Native Americans about further western expansion by the colonists. The lands west of the Allegheny Mountains were to be reserved for the Native Americans. Colonists were not even allowed to negotiate to buy land from the Indians since this had resulted in fraud in the past. The Indian nations were allowed to govern their territories with their own laws. However, the colonists argued that part of the British plan was to establish more control over the colonies by keeping their inhabitants from expanding into the newly acquired territory from France.

In order to enforce the proclamation, the British had to keep an army stationed in North America. To pay for this army and to help pay off the huge debt caused by the French and Indian War, the British government began imposing taxes. They argued that the army was there to protect the colonists. The colonists believed that it was the crown's responsibility to pay for the army, not theirs. The standing army and the taxes served to enrage the colonists and led them down the road that would eventually result in revolution and independence.

Benjamin Franklin was much more than an elder statesman. He was also a printer, author, diplomat, scientist, and inventor. His inventions include bifocals, the lightning rod, and the Franklin Stove. This painting was completed by Charles Willson Peale in 1789, one year before Franklin's death.

This engraving of the Boston Massacre was created by Paul Revere soon after the event. It is a classic example of propaganda. The inflammatory title of the engraving is "The Bloody Massacre," and it depicts a well-organized group of soldiers being spurred on by their leader to shoot into an unarmed group of colonists. This image helped stir up the colonists against the British.

CHAPTER SIX ❧
Colonial Unity

WHY DID THE COLONISTS EVENTUALLY WANT TO break away from Great Britain and form an independent country with its own laws? There is no simple answer to this question. The geographic location of the colonies was a huge factor in allowing for the independent spirit to arise. New York itself was about 3,400 miles (5,470 kilometers) away from Great Britain. This meant that sending messages and troops took quite some time. Over time, the colonies were treated with a varying degree of interest by the British government. During many years of neglect, the colonies governed themselves. This history of independent thinking embodied the American spirit.

The American colonies were independent of Great Britain in more ways than just geographically. Colonial legislatures had been given a great deal of power including the ability to muster troops, levy taxes, and pass laws. By the time the British Parliament decided to reassert its authority over the colonies after the French and Indian War, this practice of self-rule had created a group of leaders who would become the future founders of the United States of America.

Great Britain and Its Colonies

The goal of colonization for the European nations, including Great Britain, was based in mercantilism. This was the belief that the way to increase a country's wealth was through conquest or colonization. Colonies existed for the benefit of the mother country. For many years leading up to the French and Indian War, Great Britain operated under the idea of salutary neglect, which had been proposed by Sir Roger Walpole. Salutary neglect was the theory that if the British crown was lax in enforcing trade regulations with the colonies then the colonies would have a greater incentive to increase commerce. This would benefit the British by returning greater profits.

Samuel Adams was able to mobilize opposition to British actions in the colonies. He was not only one of the leaders of the Sons of Liberty, but he was also well connected, as demonstrated by his ability to influence John Adams and John Hancock. Samuel Adams was part of both Continental Congresses, and he signed the Declaration of Independence.

However, the belief that salutary neglect would work changed with the increase in troops in America after the French and Indian War. The British wanted the colonists to share more of the costs. To this end, Great Britain began instituting more laws. These laws varied from taxes to restrictions on who the colonists could trade with. The colonists did not take these laws lightly. Since the colonists had grown used to self-rule, they believed that it was their right to have a say in laws and taxes that affected them.

One year after the Proclamation of 1763 (*see* Chapter 5), the British Parliament passed a series of acts that increasingly restricted trade and taxed goods in the colonies. The Sugar Act was intended to force the colonists to buy from British sources. It charged an import tax on items such as sugar, molasses, coffee, cloth, and silk. The British navy enforced the tax. The increased cost of molasses immediately caused rum production to slow considerably. This had been a source of income for the colonies, and the decreased production had a huge effect on the colonial economy.

The Currency Act of 1764 further harmed the economy by prohibiting the colonies from creating their own currency. All currency was to be controlled by the British Parliament.

These two acts created a wave of protest among the colonists. Their reaction was based on the idea that while the Parliament did have a right to impose taxes on them, the colonists should be able to have a say. In other words, they argued for "no taxation without representation."

ARCTIC OCEAN

BERING
SEA

INUIT

N
W E
S

ALEUT

INUIT

PACIFIC

OCEAN

TLINGIT

HAIDA

TSIMSHIAN
Disputed
by Russia
and Spain

SALISH

NOOTKA

NEZ
PERCE

DENE

DOGRIB

CHIPEWYAN

CREE

BLACKFOOT

KOOTENAI

ASSINIBOINE

CROW

Hudson
Bay

INUIT

NASKAPI

MONTAGNAIS

St. Lawrence R.

BEOTHUK

MICMAC

CREE

ALGONQUIN

Quebec

ABENAKI

Halifax

Montreal

OJIBWA
(CHIPPEWA)

CHEYENNE

DAKOTA
(SIOUX)

SAUK

HURON

IROQUOIS

MOHAWK
ONONDAGA
CAYUGA
SENECA
TUSCARORA ONEIDA

Boston

NARRAGANSETT
PEQUOT

PAIUTE

SHOSHONE

PAWNEE

POMO

YOKUT

UTE

ARAPAHO

NAVAJO

PUEBLO
HOPI PUEBLO

PAPAGO

APACHE
PUEBLO

COCHIMI

PIMA

ZACATEC

OTTAWA

POTAWATOMI

IOWA

ILLINOIS

SHAWNEE

KIOWA

COMANCHE

Santa Fe

NATCHEZ

Mississippi R.

Ohio R.

ERIE

New York

SUSQUEHANNOCK

Philadelphia

Baltimore

LENNI LENAPE (DELAWARE)

POWHATAN

ATLANTIC

OCEAN

CHEROKEE

CHICKASAW

Charles Town

YAMASEE

CREEK

CHOCTAW

St. Augustine

Rio Grande R.

New Orleans

CALUSA

LUCAYO

SEMINOLE

British

COAHUILTEC

Gulf of
Mexico

Havana

CIBONEY

SUB TAINO

ARAWAK

ARAWAK
TAINO

British

ARAWAK
CARIB

Zacatecas

TOLTEC

Guadalajara

Mexico City

NAHUATL
(AZTEC)

Acapulco

Vera Cruz

MIXTEC

Mérida

MAYA

ZAPOTEC

CARIBBEAN SEA

MISKITO

Santo Domingo

French

French

Dutch

British

CUNA

GUAYMI

Spanish
British
French
Russian

0   500   1,000 Miles
0   500   1,000 Kilometers

This map portrays North America in 1775. The British population was concentrated mostly along the Atlantic Ocean, and the Spanish had their major cities in Mexico. By this time, the French had been pushed out of the region and only held small areas in the Caribbean Sea.

Committees of Correspondence

In order to help organize the protests, the colonists established communication through committees of correspondence. At this time, the main way to share information between colonies was by letter carried by couriers. Networks of these couriers were called committees of correspondence. They were created by colonial assemblies, local governments, and secret organizations such as the Sons of Liberty. These committees were responsible for sending news to other groups and colonies to help organize efforts as they fought common problems.

In 1764, the first formal committee of correspondence was created with the idea of instigating unrest and creating organized opposition to the Currency Act and other British acts. The primary goal was to organize boycotts of British-imported goods, an action that had a huge impact on the business of British merchants.

In 1765, Parliament created even more restrictive laws. The Quartering Act forced homeowners to house soldiers and officers when there was no room in the barracks. The homeowners would be responsible for providing each soldier with not only a bed but also food and drink. That same year, another law was passed that increased both unity and resistance among the colonists: the Stamp Act.

New York created a committee of correspondence focused on fighting the Stamp Act in order to create resistance to the taxes. This led to the Stamp Act Congress that met in protest of the latest measures passed by Parliament.

Up until 1773, committees were created for specific purposes and were dissolved as issues were dealt with. However, the problems were deepening to the point that by 1773, a special committee of correspondence was created by the Virginia House of Burgesses. Its purpose was to gain support for a permanent means of unity among the colonies against the increasing incursions by the British crown.

British Acts That Led to Rebellion

Date	Act	Explanation
1763	Proclamation of 1763	The Proclamation of 1763 was passed after the signing of the Treaty of Paris that ended the French and Indian War. It did not allow any settlements west of the Allegheny Mountains and created new governing structures. Its stated purpose was to keep the colonists safe while calming fears on the part of the Native Americans about losing their land. The enforcement of this proclamation led to more British troops being left in colonial America.
1764	Currency Act of 1764	The Currency Act made it so that paper money could no longer be used as legal tender in the colonies. Also, colonies could no longer print their own paper money. This hurt the colonial economies.
1765	Quartering Act	According to the Quartering Act, all colonial legislatures had to provide food and lodging for British soldiers stationed in the colonies.
1765	Stamp Act	The Stamp Act placed a tax on numerous items including legal documents, licenses, contracts, newspapers, and playing cards. Even though these were taxes already being paid in Great Britain, they were new to the colonies. Colonists argued that they had no representation in Parliament, and the act caused major resistance in the colonies.
1767	Townshend Acts	Wanting to increase the power of the British Parliament and royal officials, Charles Townshend had a series of acts passed that increased existing taxes or added new ones. The acts also provided more control over the royal officials in America because their salaries would now be paid directly by the crown.
1773	Tea Act	Even though no new taxes were created with the Tea Act, it did require the extra tea from the East India Company to be sold at a cheaper price in the colonies. This would in turn hurt local merchants who sold tea. This act led directly to the Boston Tea Party.
1774	Intolerable Acts	Series of laws was passed by the British Parliament after the Boston Tea Party. These acts were very strict and included the closing of the Boston Harbor. The acts served to increase the support for independence from Great Britain.

Through the committees, the colonies were able to make plans for the First Continental Congress in 1774.

Committees of correspondence were again used during the Second Continental Congress that met in 1775. They shared information about the events of the Congress. They were also important in getting

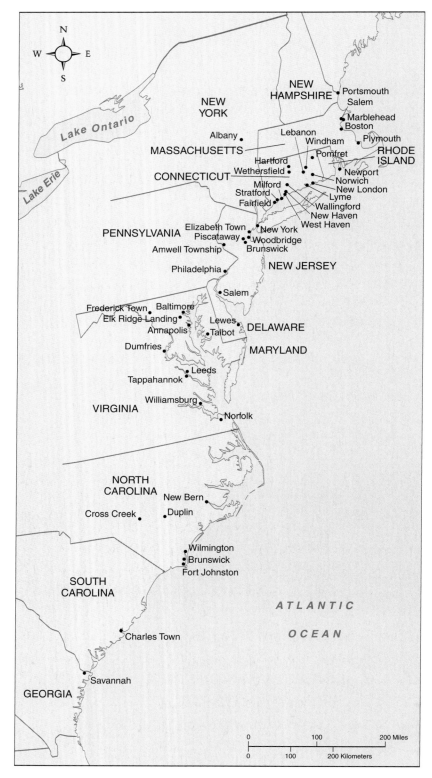

information into French hands since the colonists hoped that the French would support their bid for independence.

The Stamp Act and the Sons of Liberty

The 1765 Stamp Act caused the colonists to pay for stamps on all legal documents, permits, newspapers, and playing cards, among other items. Its purpose was to help pay for the cost of the troops that the British had stationed in America. The act was a huge cause of discontent throughout the colonies because of its widespread effect and the

This map of the demonstrations against the Stamp Act in 1765 shows the widespread nature of such uprisings throughout the colonies. The Sons of Liberty led many of the demonstrations. These and other forms of protest formed the foundation for the organized resistance against Great Britain that eventually would lead to open rebellion and, finally, self-rule.

direct nature of the tax. With an indirect tax, the money given to the government is hidden from the public. However, with a direct tax such as the Stamp Act, it was obvious how much money was being paid to the government. This angered the colonists, who did not believe it necessary to pay this new tax when they did not have the necessary representation to protect their interests in Parliament.

In 1765, a group of nine individuals in Boston (who called themselves the Loyal Nine) joined to fight against the Stamp Act. As more people joined the group, they became known as the Sons of Liberty. This group, along with the Daughters of Liberty, acted covertly to fight the Stamp Act. They committed acts of protest such as burning royal officials in effigy. They put pressure on stamp distributors to resign and persuaded merchants to stop importing British products, as a form of protest. They had many in the press behind them, and their deeds were printed in papers across the colonies.

By 1766, the Sons of Liberty had been so effective that many of the royal officials went into hiding. Even though officials from each colony would eventually meet to form the resistance and fight the British, colonial unity began with independent nongovernmental groups like the Sons of Liberty.

Stamp Act Congress

Opposition to the Stamp Act was such that many acts of violence began occurring throughout the colonies. Some, however, tried to take a more reasonable approach to fighting the act. Patrick Henry authored resolutions against the act that were adopted by the Virginia House of Burgesses. James Otis of Massachusetts used the committee of correspondence to get the colonies to meet in opposition to the act. This resulted in the Stamp Act Congress, which met in

Patrick Henry's Fifth Resolution ৶

Patrick Henry was one of the most radical revolutionaries in colonial America. His famous speech that ended with the line "I know not what course others may take; but as for me, give me liberty or give me death!" was one of the main reasons why Virginia decided to build up its military in 1775 and prepare for war. Starting ten years before this speech, Henry was a key figure in beginning the move toward independence. He proposed the Virginia Stamp Act Resolutions to argue against taxation without representation. His fifth proposal, which passed at first but was quickly withdrawn once he was no longer present, argued that only the General Assembly of Virginia had the right to tax the colonists.

Patrick Henry was a radical for his time. He was only twenty-nine when he was elected to the Virginia House of Burgesses, and he spoke publicly against Great Britain, something many people were afraid to do for fear of being labeled traitors.

New York City on October 7, 1765. Nine of the thirteen colonies attended, including Massachusetts, Connecticut, Rhode Island, New York, New Jersey, Pennsylvania, Delaware, Maryland, and South Carolina.

The result of the congress was the creation of the Declaration of Rights and Grievances. The fourteen points of this declaration were created mainly by John Dickinson of Pennsylvania. The declaration argued that it was not the right of the British government to impose taxes on all colonies. Instead, colonies should determine taxes through their own legislative bodies. The delegates also agreed to restrict British imports and to organize protests and resistance. Despite their protests, the delegates did pledge their loyalty to the king and Great Britain. In the end, the British Parliament repealed the Stamp Act.

However, the fact that the Stamp Act Congress was an official meeting of the colonies in protest to an act from Great Britain was an important step toward colonial unity. After the congress disbanded, the committee of correspondence continued to keep the colonies unified.

Increasing Tensions

In 1767, Parliament reduced taxes in England. The British, led by Charles Townshend, decided to force the American colonists to make up the difference by increasing their taxes. Taxes were imposed on imported items such as tea, glass, and paper in order to pay for British colonial officials. These officials would be independent from the colonial legislatures.

In response, the colonists took even more organized action than they had during the Stamp Act and hurt British merchants by ceasing to buy British goods. By 1770 all the Townshend Acts, except for the tax on tea, were repealed due to pressure from the merchants.

Yet the opposition to the acts had increased tensions in the colonies. This led to an event that became known as the Boston Massacre. On March 5, 1770, a group of colonists were taunting British soldiers. Verbal hostilities increased, and a British sentry called for help. A group of soldiers led by Captain Thomas Preston arrived on the scene and was surrounded. At some point a musket was fired into the crowd, and this was followed by more shots. The event left several colonists wounded and five dead, including African American Crispus Attucks.

Many questions still remain about this event. One thing is certain, however: The colonists were able to use the Boston Massacre as a rallying cry for those protesting and resisting British actions.

Boston Tea Party

In 1773, Parliament passed a Tea Act. Although it actually resulted in lower costs for the colonists, this act also told the colonists from whom they had to buy tea. Because of this, the colonists actively opposed the act. This opposition surprised the British. It also led to the infamous Boston Tea Party. On December 16, 1773, members of the

Sons of Liberty dressed as Mohawk Indians and dumped 342 crates of tea into Boston Harbor.

Many of the colonists did not agree with this action but that did not matter. The British responded by closing Boston Harbor and enacting other restrictive acts nicknamed the "Intolerable Acts." One of those acts, called the Massachusetts Government Act, made all government positions in Massachusetts appointed, thus removing the colony's right to self-rule. Further, the governor could move any trial to Great Britain. These acts caused sympathy for Massachusetts and helped to unify the colonies in fear of what could happen to them.

First Continental Congress

After the Intolerable Acts were passed, committees of correspondence helped organize the First Continental Congress. This was a huge event in the move toward independence. The congress met at Carpenter's Hall in Philadelphia, Pennsylvania, from September 5, 1774, until October 26, 1774.

Twelve of the thirteen colonies were represented by fifty-five delegates, with only Georgia holding back. Important individuals who attended the congress included John Adams, Samuel Adams, John Dickinson, Patrick Henry, John Jay, and George Washington. The goal of the Continental Congress was not to demand independence but instead to find a way to get the British government to rescind its unpopular acts and to gain a better voice in the London assembly.

The First Continental Congress resulted in some major actions. One of the first things to be resolved was how the colonies would act toward the British. Pennsylvania delegate Joseph Galloway wanted to create an American parliament as a means of compromise to help work with the British. However, the more radical elements of the congress would not consider this plan and instead adopted the Suffolk Resolves. These were created by representatives from the Boston and surrounding Suffolk County areas. The most radical of the resolves was the statement that

> no obedience is due . . . but that they be rejected as the attempts of a wicked administration to enslave America. . . . That whereas our enemies have flattered themselves that they shall make an easy prey of this numerous, brave and hardy people, from an apprehension that they are unacquainted with military discipline; we . . . advise . . . that those who now hold commissions . . . do use their utmost diligence to acquaint themselves with the art of war as soon as possible. . . .

This painting depicts delegates to the First Continental Congress at Carpenter's Hall in Philadelphia. All of the colonies except Georgia, which had just recently been founded, sent delegates. The delegates met for a month and a half in 1774.

The Continental Congress also created the Association, which promoted a boycott of British goods. This included bans on importing, exporting, and consuming items created or provided by Great Britain. Committees were to enforce this by publicly revealing names of merchants who did not follow the Association's bans. They would also confiscate any items they found that broke the boycott.

Finally, the Continental Congress created the Declaration of Rights and Grievances, which listed the complaints of the colonists against King George III, based on the Suffolk Resolves. One of the important sections of the declaration stated

> [t]hat the foundation of English liberty, and of all free government, is a right in the people to participate in their legislative council: and as the English colonists are not represented, and from their local and other circumstances, cannot properly be represented in the British parliament, they are entitled to a free and exclusive power of legislation in their several provincial legislatures, where their right of representation can alone be preserved.

When the congress adjourned, it agreed to meet again the following year if the complaints presented to the king were not addressed. This resulted in the Second Continental Congress in May 1775, after the battles of Lexington and Concord had occurred.

Second Continental Congress

In April 1775, skirmishes occurred at Lexington and Concord. The British had been sent to destroy stockpiles of weapons that the colonists had been collecting at Concord, Massachusetts. They were also sent to arrest John Hancock and Samuel Adams, who were in Lexington. Colonial leaders received a warning of the impending attack. Paul Revere arranged a signal with which to warn those in Concord and Lexington: He would put one lantern in the Old North Church steeple in Boston if the British were attacking by land and two lanterns if by sea. He hung two lanterns, alerting Hancock and Adams to flee by land, and giving the colonists enough time to remove many of the weapons. "Minutemen," or colonial militias, attacked the British on their way back from Boston. These were the first battles of the upcoming American Revolution.

In response, the Second Continental Congress was convened in Philadelphia on May 10, 1775. John Hancock was elected as the presiding officer of the congress. All thirteen colonies sent delegates, such as Benjamin Franklin, Thomas Jefferson, John Adams, Samuel Adams, and Richard Henry Lee. Just as with the first congress, the goal of the meeting was not to break from Great Britain but to heal the rift between the two countries. The delegates considered themselves loyal subjects of the king but did not believe that their rights as Englishmen were being respected.

Thomas Paine wrote a pamphlet in 1776 called *Common Sense* that spoke out against British rule and argued for colonial independence. This pamphlet was extremely important in gaining popular support for the Revolutionary War. Nevertheless, only about one-third of the population openly supported the rebellion, one-third was neutral, and the last third was actually loyal to the crown.

The Second Continental Congress was an extremely important body in the Revolutionary War. Its members assumed control of the army that was camped outside of Boston. George Washington was chosen as the commander in chief of the Continental Army. In addition to his fighting experience, Washington was chosen because, as John Adams argued, he was a southerner and would help shore up southern support for the fight against the British.

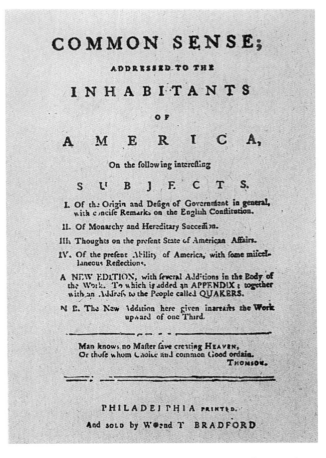

Thomas Paine's Common Sense *was hugely popular, with over 120,000 copies in circulation within three months of its publication. In this pamphlet, Paine laid out the case against continued association with Britain in terms that all could understand: "I challenge the warmest advocate for reconciliation [with Britain] to show a single advantage that this continent can reap."*

The Continental Army under the command of George Washington was encamped at Valley Forge in Pennsylvania for six months, beginning in December 1777. That winter, the soldiers struggled to overcome extreme cold, starvation, and despair. After four months, Baron von Steuben arrived to train the troops. His training, along with better weather and fresh supplies, helped reinvigorate the army.

In order to pay the army and finance the war, the congress borrowed and issued paper certificates. However, the congress had money problems throughout the course of the war. This can be seen by the dismal state the military found itself in while stationed at Valley Forge, Pennsylvania, during the winter of 1777–1778.

At the beginning of the conflict, the Continental Congress issued two statements to explain their reasons for fighting against the British while still asserting their loyalty. They created the Olive Branch Petition. This explained that they were loyal to the king but did not believe that Parliament and the ministers had the right to take the actions they had against the colonies. They also released the Declaration of the Causes and Necessity of Taking Up Arms. This actually demanded that the problems be rectified otherwise a fight for independence might be a possibility.

Declaration of Independence

Since the British did not meet the demands of the colonists, Richard Henry Lee created a resolution in June 1776 asking for independence from Great Britain. Congress adopted the resolution and appointed a five-man committee to create a declaration of independence. The main text of the declaration was drafted by Thomas Jefferson between June 11 and June 28, 1776. He was heavily influenced by the Virginia Declaration of Rights. This had been written by George Mason shortly before Jefferson wrote his declaration and was adopted by the Virginia Constitutional Convention on June 12, 1776. The Virginia Declaration of Rights included the following passage, which was used by Thomas Jefferson as he wrote his declaration:

> That all men are by nature equally free and independent and have certain inherent rights, of which, when they enter into a state of society, they cannot, by any compact, deprive or divest their posterity; namely, the enjoyment of life and liberty, with the means of acquiring and possessing property, and pursuing and obtaining happiness and safety.

Compare this to these remarks in Jefferson's opening paragraph:

> We hold these Truths to be self-evident, that all Men are created equal, that they are endowed by their Creator with certain unalienable Rights, that among these are Life, Liberty and the Pursuit of Happiness.

Both of these declarations were based on the political philosophy that had been written many years previously by John Locke and Jean Jacques Rousseau. Locke argued that government should be limited and that it was a contract that could be dissolved if it did not protect people's natural rights to life, liberty, and property. Rousseau argued that government is only acceptable if it is established by the "consent of the governed." Therefore, a society must continually ensure that leaders are living up to their end of the social contract.

Thomas Jefferson was the author of the Declaration of Independence and the second president of the United States. He was also an inventor, diplomat, educator, and architect. He is called the "Father of the University of Virginia," because he designed many of its buildings and its course of study.

Once the rights and liberties that should be afforded citizens were expressed by Jefferson, he went into a list of grievances that the colonists had against the king. Even though this was called a declaration of independence, there was still the hope by many that this would cause the crown to change its policies, and that England and its colonies could then reconcile.

Other Actions of the Continental Congress

The Second Continental Congress was also responsible for trying to get foreign nations involved in the Revolution. In 1778, the Franco-American Alliance was created. During the Revolutionary War, France helped out the colonists by sending supplies, weapons, and experienced military officers such as the Marquis de Lafayette. France's assistance led to the victory at Yorktown in 1781 where the British surrendered to the colonists, ending the Revolution. The support of the French also helped America gain recognition of its independence, established by the Treaty of Versailles, signed in 1783.

One other issue that took up much of the time at the Second Continental Congress was dealing with the differences between the needs and interests of the northern and southern colonies, which were causing conflicts even at this early date. These would not be resolved until the American Civil War that began in 1861.

In November 1777, the Articles of Confederation were adopted to form the basis for the new nation. The states ratified the Articles in 1781. The Articles created a loose confederation of states that gave each state sovereign power. It gave the combined government very little power. Eventually, the inability of the central government to collect taxes and pass laws led to the creation of the U.S. Constitution, which is still followed by the United States today.

Timeline ≈

1215	Magna Carta is signed, limiting the power of the monarch.
1298	Marco Polo writes *The Travels of Marco Polo*.
1492	Christopher Columbus tries to sail from Spain to China but finds the Americas.
1607	Jamestown is founded by the English.
1608	Quebec is founded by the French.
1620	The Mayflower Compact is signed, becoming the first written agreement for a government in the New World. The Massachusetts Bay Colony is founded.
1623	New Hampshire is founded by the English.
1625	New Amsterdam is founded by the Dutch.
1628	King Charles I signs the Petition of Right requiring the king to obey the laws.
1634	Connecticut is founded by the English.
1636	Rhode Island is founded by the English.
1638	Delaware is founded by the Swedes.
1639	The Fundamental Orders of Connecticut are created.
1643	New England Confederation is formed.
1649	An Act Concerning Religion, or The Maryland Toleration Act, is enacted.
1660	The Restoration of King Charles II of England takes place.
1663	Carolina is founded by the English.
1664	James, Duke of York, captures New Amsterdam and renames it New York. New Jersey is founded by the English.
1682	Pennsylvania is founded by the English.
1688	The Glorious Revolution begins. The English Bill of Rights is passed.
1732	Georgia is founded by the English.
1735	John Peter Zenger is found innocent of libel, beginning the American tradition of freedom of the press.
1754	Albany Plan of Union is proposed by Benjamin Franklin in order to create a central government over the colonies. It is rejected by the colonial legislatures and King George II.
1754–1763	The French and Indian War occurs. The English win and leave garrisons in the colonies.
1763	Pontiac's Rebellion occurs, resulting in the Proclamation of 1763.

Glossary ⌘

alliance	When two or more groups of individuals agree to unite for varying reasons, including mutual protection and economic interests.
Black Death	Name given by Europeans to the bubonic plague, a disease that killed huge numbers of people in repeated epidemics.
boycott	When a group of individuals agrees to stop buying from or associating with a business or, in some cases, an entire country.
conquistadors	Spanish soldiers during the colonial era.
Continental Congress	Two meetings of the English colonies held in 1774 and 1775. The colonies met to discuss unpopular British actions and make plans for mutual protection. The Second Continental Congress led to the fight for independence.
effigy	A likeness of a person, for example a king or governor.
encomienda	The system the Spanish used to establish control in their lands. This system gave individuals control over a territory where they had the ability to tax the inhabitants in exchange for providing them with military protection.
English Common Law	The body of laws developed between the thirteenth and the seventeenth centuries in England that guaranteed English liberties. The laws protected Englishmen and their property. The U.S. Constitution was based in part on English Common Law.
Far East	A term used to describe the countries in East and Southeast Asia.
freeman	Someone who is free; not a slave or indentured servant.
Iroquois Nation	Also known as the League of the Five Nations and the Iroquois Confederacy. Many different Iroquois tribes came together under a mutual government. Their unity provided them with mutual protection and organization.
Jesuit	A Roman Catholic religious order founded by St. Ignatius Loyola. Many of the missionaries who came to the Americas to convert the native populations were from the Jesuit order.
joint-stock company	A private company whereby investors could pool their money in order to back trading ventures. An example would be the Jamestown venture that was funded by the Virginia Company.

libel	A false statement about someone that is printed and hurts that person's reputation.
Mayflower Compact	The first independent governmental agreement made in the New World. English colonists who had arrived in what would become Massachusetts agreed to the Mayflower Compact to help them set up a government.
mission	A settlement, usually built around a church and school, established to convert people in the area to Christianity.
missionaries	Individuals who attempt to spread their religious beliefs by interacting with those who do not share their beliefs. Missionaries traveled to the Americas to spread Christianity.
Northwest Passage	European explorers attempted to find this commercial route that connected the Atlantic and Pacific oceans to reach the Far East. They were unsuccessful.
Pilgrims	English religious separatists who broke away from the Church of England. They traveled to and settled in North America in the 1600s in search of a place where they could freely practice their religion.
privateer	A private ship or vessel that is armed and acts secretly under the direction of a foreign power. In other words, a state-sponsored pirate.
Puritans	Calvinists who felt that the Church of England was too much like the Roman Catholic Church and wanted a purer religion. Many of them immigrated to North America and many of the earlier colonies were primarily Puritans.
smallpox	A serious and sometimes fatal disease that is extremely infectious. It is characterized by bumps that appear on the body.
Sons of Liberty	Secret groups of individuals who led the resistance against the British for acts that they felt were unfair, especially the Stamp Act. Two of the most famous Sons of Liberty members were Samuel Adams and Paul Revere.
trading posts	Places where European powers traded with the Native Americans.
viceroyalty	The area under the rule of the viceroy, or the representative of the king or queen.

For More Information ❧

The books and Web sites listed below contain information about the government of North America. Most of the books were written especially for young adults. The others will not be too difficult for most young readers. The Web site addresses were accurate when this book was written, but remember that Web sites and their addresses change frequently. Your librarian can help you find additional resources.

Books

Ciment, James, ed. *Colonial America: An Encyclopedia of Social, Political, Cultural, and Economic History*. 5 vols. Armonk, NY: M.E. Sharpe, 2006.

Hakim, Joy. *The First Americans*. New York: Oxford University Press, 2003.

Middleton, Richard. *Colonial America: A History, 1565–1776*. Boston: Blackwell, 2002.

Philbrick, Nathaniel. *Mayflower: A Story of Courage, Community, and War*. New York: Viking, 2006.

Rosen, Daniel. *New Beginnings: Jamestown and the Virginia Colony 1607–1699*. Washington, DC: National Geographic, 2005.

Web Sites

http://memory.loc.gov/learn/features/timeline/amrev/amrev.html
The American Memory Project of the Library of Congress includes numerous primary and secondary sources about the American Revolution, 1763–1783.

http://americanhistory.about.com/library/charts/blcolonial13.htm
The About.com American History page provides a chart with links for further information for each of the thirteen colonies. Other resources about the colonial era are also available on this site, including timelines and quizzes.

http://www.dinsdoc.com/colonial-1.htm
Dinsmore Documentation has a large collection of online texts about colonial history. All of the texts were published before 1923 and are in the public domain.

http://www.pbs.org/benfranklin/
PBS has created a site devoted entirely to Benjamin Franklin. Included are timelines, primary and secondary sources, and biographical information.

http://www.mayflowerhistory.com/

This site provides a background to the *Mayflower* along with primary texts from the pilgrims, history, and genealogy information.

http://www.frenchandindianwar250.org/

The French and Indian War Commemoration site was created to remember the war 250 years later. It includes a wealth of information, including places to visit, timelines, primary sources, and more.

Primary Source List ∾

Chapter 3   p. 39 "Journal of the First Voyage of Christopher Columbus, 1492–1493." In *The Northmen, Columbus, and Cabot, 985–1503*, edited by Julius Olsen and Edward Gaylord Bourne, pp. 114, 145–146, 182. New York: Scribner's, 1906.

Chapter 4   p. 54 Mayflower Compact, in *Colonial America: An Encyclopedia of Social, Political, Cultural, and Economic History*, edited by James Ciment. Vol. 5. Armonk, NY: M.E. Sharpe, 2006.

pp. 56-57 Fundamental Orders of Connecticut, in *Colonial America: An Encyclopedia of Social, Political, Cultural, and Economic History*, edited by James Ciment. Vol. 5. Armonk, NY: M.E. Sharpe, 2006.

p. 58 Act Concerning Religion, in *Colonial America: An Encyclopedia of Social, Political, Cultural, and Economic History*, edited by James Ciment. Vol. 5. Armonk, NY: M.E. Sharpe, 2006.

Chapter 6   pp. 85-86 Suffolk Resolves and Agreement by Continental Congress, September 1774. Available at the Library of Congress Web site at http://memory.loc.gov/learn/features/timeline/amrev/rebelln/suffolk.html

p. 89 Virginia Declaration of Rights. Available at the Web site of the Constitution Society at http://www.constitution.org/bcp/virg_dor.htm. Distributed by the Cybercasting Services Division of the National Public Telecomputing Network (NPTN).

p. 89 Declaration of Independence, in *Colonial America: An Encyclopedia of Social, Political, Cultural, and Economic History*, edited by James Ciment. Vol. 5. Armonk, NY: M.E. Sharpe, 2006.

Index ☙